IN A MIRROR
Dimly

A MEMOIR

ELLEN SATINOFF

Copyright © 2025 Ellen Satinoff
All Rights Reserved

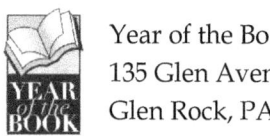
Year of the Book
135 Glen Avenue
Glen Rock, PA 17327

ISBN: 978-1-64649-490-3 (paperback)
ISBN: 978-1-64649-491-0 (ebook)

This book is memoir. It reflects the author's present recollections of experiences over time. Some names and characteristics have been changed, some events have been compressed, and some dialogue has been recreated.

Printed in the United States of America

Contents

Preface i

Queens

A Bride Doll and a Jungle 3
Mea Culpa 5
Frozen at the Altar 6
Miss Evelyn and a Port Wine Stain 7
Bedstands and Barstools 8
God's Name is Spot 11
We Gotta Get Outta This Place 13
I Dream of Jennie 14
Show Me the Money 15
Put on a Happy Face 16
The Cure Could Kill You 17
The Bus Ride That Wasn't 17
Silver, Not Gold 18
Here's to You, Miss Evelyn 19

Long Island – West Islip

Van Buren—Not the President 23
The Cloud Without a Silver Lining 24
Onion Soup 24
Another Time, Another Jungle 25
Words That Hurt 26
We're Gonna Be Loaded 27
The Tank 28
Boston Bound 28

Long Island – North Babylon

It's All Ours 33
Baubles, Bangles, and Beads 33
Fun for Free 34
Rice and Coffee 36
Chinese Red 37

A Tidal Wave in the Dance Studio	39
Little Rockefellers	40
I Will Kill You	41
Can't Rain (or Snow) on Our Parade	42
Fire and Ice	43
Streams of Adventure	47
Martians and the Blessed Virgin Mary	47
Kissing Cousins	50
Wedded "Bliss"	52
Collecting for Leukemia	53
Mea Culpa, Part 2	54
The Bride of Christ	57
An Unholy Ending	59
Tempting the Priest	60
Music Lessons	61
That Which Doesn't Kill You	66

The Manhattan Experience

50 Carmine	71
Abacus and Espresso	74
Baldwin and Remington	75
Into the Catacomb	76
A Kidney and a Radio	77
Whiskey and Diamonds	77
Water Closet Willies	81
Old World Meets New World	82
The Lower East Side	83
Ballet and Bali	86
Carp and Pagodas	86

The Bronx

Bronx Bombshell	91
She Got Her Wings	93
Our Little Secret	94
Bambole and Laundry	95
A War Heroine	96

California 1

Come Fly with Me 99
Teacups and Whales 101

Deer Park Elementary

Curlicues and Cruelty 107
That's the Way the Cookie… er… Cake Crumbles 108
The Judas Kiss 109
My Heroic Enemy 110
Comrade Satinoff 112
Russian Princesses 113
Miss Carmody 114
The Unthinkable 116
Kate Smith and Cigarettes 116
Pickles and Eggs in Ancient Egypt 117
The Big F 119
Finally Made It to the Top 119
So I'm a Drug Addict 120
Blood and Milk 121
I Saved the Day! 122
Broadway Babies 123

On the Road

Hitchin' a Ride 129
North by Northeast 129
Submarines and Whale Teeth 131
The Bad Old Days 131
A Clown Car and Hobo Ham 134
Barron's in the Pines 136
A Crustacean Education 136
Conquering the Cliffs 137
Bologna in the Biscayne 139
Ambrosia It Ain't 142
Bay of Fundy 143
Back to Home Base 144

The Academy

Dressed, but Not to Kill 147

The Breakfast of Champions 149
Spoon Fed 149
There Will Be Nun of That 150

On the Road... Again

Florida Bound 155
The Steamy, Stormy Smoky Mountains 155
Rain and Pancakes 156
A Rocky Experience 158
Florida, Finally 159

Leaving, Not on a Jet Plane

This Thing Is Not Like the Other 163
It's Really Happening 165
Well, We Made It 167
Meeting New People 168
A Blazing Birthday 170
Old Ladies and a Donkey 171
Mine Shafts and Donkey Meat 174
A Rootin' Tootin' Good Time 177
But Yes, We Have No... Roaches 179
Tawk the Tawk 180
Tripping the Light Fantastic 182
A Pernicious Plot 182
...To Soothe the Savage Breast 184
Minks, Appliances, and Fireworks 184

You Can Go Home Again

Upping Sticks 189
A Bittersweet Reunion 191
Settling In 192
Jukeboxes, Smokes, and Taps 194

The Hospital and First Love

Sick, with Dread 199
On a Rollercoaster 200
Thunderstruck 203
Getting to Know You 204
Falling Deeper and Deeper… 207

…And Hitting Bottom 208
Comes the Reaper 209

Ossining

Bye-bye Bronx 213
Our New Digs 214
Getting Our Bearings 216
Ne Suis Pas une Boulangère 217
A Sorry Souffle 218
Just Keep it to Ourselves 219

California 2

Flying Solo 223
The Best Laid Plans 225
Alone Again, Unnaturally 227
A Whole Lotta Shakin' Goin' On 228
Up, Up, and Away 229
It's a Happenin' Scene, Man 231

Ossining Redux

On the Sidelines 237
Strollin' Along 237
Rats! Foiled Again 238
An Education Revelation 239
Monet or Midnight Cowboy and a Men's Motel 240
The Park Lane Hotel 241
Toe Shoes and Toilet Plungers 242
Louie, Louie 244
It's a Grand Union 245
She Ain't No Friend of Mine 246
A Hot Tomato 247
The Portuguese 248
A Close Encounter 251
Reading, Writing, Refund 251
Part of the Family 252
That's a Wrap 253
Genoa or Hard? 254
A Rose is a Rose 254

One Foot into My Future... 255
Come Blow Your Horn.. 257
An Unmet Expectation 258
Sneaking Off 260
Them Tires is Smokin' – and so were we.. 260
A House Divided 262
Moving On Up... 263

1972

Pete.. 269
It's in the Cards... 270
It's All Fun and Games Until.. 270
Happy New Year... 272
Meeting Viola... 275
A Ring and Roses 276
Wedding Plans 277
I'm a Good Little Soldier 279
The Day Arrives 281

Epilogue.. 285

"For now we see in a mirror dimly, but then face to face." I Cor. 13:12a

Until I began writing, my past was a blurry pastiche of memories, played out in my mind like a slide show, but with the slides out of order. *Here I am at 15, this is me at 6, one time when I was 12...* There was no coherence or sense of organization. I had no understanding that these individual, transient images were the key to who I was — am — as a grownup. I was a lonely, scared child who grew into an insecure, unhappy, and often times angry adult.

The quote from I Corinthians, written by the apostle Paul, perfectly sums up my earthly experience *and* my heavenly hope. Paul spoke of when Christians will see Jesus face to face, with perfect clarity, since as earthly beings we can only see Him in an unclear manner. I believe Paul chose this analogy, apropos for the time, because in antiquity mirrors were made of metal, which distorted images.

It is also apropos to my experiences as a child, which grew me into a grownup with a distorted perception of reality. It took years of therapy, traveling the countless dead ends of my childhood, to arrive at a destination marked by discernment, acceptance, and finally, forgiveness.

My mother and I were estranged for over 20 years. A little before her death she agreed to see me — I suspect it was because she knew she didn't have much time left on this earth. I was able to visit with her a few times before she became bedridden, and then a handful of times after. I was able to tell her "I love you," even as she insisted that things between us "had had to be that way," whatever that meant. More importantly, by the grace of God, because He forgives me my failings and shortcomings, I was able to forgive her. I mourn her passing to this day, but oftentimes in the sense that I miss the mother she *could* have been, the mother I *might* have had.

Inevitably, my story is also her story. Her childhood was marked by constant anxiety, abuse, poverty, and violence. Not surprisingly, when I became a parent the cycle repeated itself.

It is my prayer and fervent hope that through this account my children will see me not "dimly," but with clarity and understanding. It is for them – Joan, Adam, Daniel, and Joey – that I write this, and to them that I dedicate it.

Queens

A Bride Doll and a Jungle

"Don't eat those," my mother said curtly. I was squatted unsteadily at the bottom of the stairs over a disheveled pile of paint chips, which looked to my four-year-old eyes like a drift of lead-based snowflakes. They were white, irregular, and ragged around the edges, but pure and clean. Absorbed by this tiny, private discovery, I did not notice the denuded patch of wall above that stood as a sad testament to the maintenance of our building.

My mother, my sister Paula, and I lived in Queens, NY, in an apartment situated over a dry cleaner, one of many in a row of storefronts embellished with sidewalk detritus. Tucked away between plate glass windows was a splintery wooden door that stood unobtrusively, almost embarrassed by its mean existence. This was the entrance to our home. Upon entering, one was confronted with a mountain of steps — straight up, challenging, dauntingly dim. The landing was tiled with scuffed green linoleum barely pretending to be marble, and doors leading to two apartments.

Our neighbors, John and Dolores, were young and newly married. I don't remember John, but Dolores' name sounded so exotic to me, especially if you dragged out the middle syllable. *Doloooores*. And she looked exotic too, with pale olive skin and shiny black hair that barely grazed her shoulders. Her long, finely filed fingernails were painted with clear polish up near the moon of the nail, and came to a shocking, sensuous red at the point. When I visited her she breezed back and forth in the little rooms of her tiny apartment, performing some newly assumed wifely duty, all the while talking about nothing memorable in an absentminded but good-natured way. She seemed always to be smiling. During her soliloquy she would pat my head or throw me an offhand glance. And I, her grateful and obeisant audience, applauded her performance not with gesture but with rapt attention.

My best visits with Dolores were the ones during which she let me play with her bride doll that was swathed in billowy layers of white chiffon and which stood alone in expectant, virginal attention on the bedroom dresser. Dolores' chattering faded away as I timorously stroked the doll's shiny ebony curls, made the slightest adjustment to her veil, and gently tugged a crease from the skirt. Vacant glass eyes of blue stared unblinkingly at me as I furled the lush fringe of black lashes framing them.

Unrequited as it was, I loved that doll for her beauty and innocence, her porcelain serenity. Only one door away, her world was completely different from my own. Young love and airy lace curtains blocked the grimy view of the coarse brick wall right outside the one window.

The door on the right led to our apartment. Straight through, one was greeted by a black steel table and four chairs covered with padded vinyl. The tabletop was black laminate with irregular white lines slashed through it, as though a feral cat had clawed its way across the surface. The table and chairs stood off-center in the kitchen, trying to hide their own ugliness.

Behind them the sink, narrow white porcelain stove, and refrigerator were in a row, culinary soldiers at attention. The room was devoid of architectural ornamentation, but my mother remedied that by putting her considerable artistic talents to work. Of all the possible scenes to grace the plaster canvas of our walls, my mother chose — perhaps tellingly — to paint a jungle.

A lion stared from behind giant fronds. Monkeys sat on branches, their tails hanging down in inverted question marks. Flora abounded, germinated from the fertile soil of my mother's imagination.

Usually people escape to their homes from the jungle of the outside world. We had the jungle in our house.

Mea Culpa

My mother's brother, Bobby, lived with us. Well, when he was between girlfriends. He was indecently handsome and had the physique of a bodybuilder, which he showed off with barely disguised pride in white tee shirts that stretched across his muscular chest and arms. Deep blue denim jeans cuffed at the bottom and black boots completed his customary dress. A shock of thick black hair was combed to the side but invariably fell over his right eye when the Brylcreem gave out.

He drove a motorcycle and often ate a large steak, cooked rare, and three runny eggs for breakfast. Even sitting still he gave the impression that at any random moment he might spontaneously combust. At the tender age of four, I already understood he was a person worth giving a wide berth.

For all that, though, he was magnetic. The force of his personality was compelling despite the palpable aura of threat and danger that he emanated. Bobby was forever rushing home from his plumbing job to clean up, only to run out just as quickly to jump on his bike and pick up one of his many dates.

His one physical flaw was a discernable limp, the result of a terrible biking accident that almost cost him his life. He lost part of his leg above the ankle, making him seem off balance, but not vulnerable. The story goes that he was in the Navy, and while motoring cross-country to report to his California base he only got as far as the Midwest when he was hit by a truck and dragged a good way under its wheel. His condition was so precarious that the Red Cross paid for my grandmother to fly out to what was presumed to be a last visit with her son. His stubborn personality asserted itself, however, and despite the odds, he survived.

After a long recuperation he was sent to Florida for rehab, where he strengthened his damaged body by swimming and taking up judo.

Aside from the limp, his only souvenir from Florida was a black belt in Judo and a belt that he hand-carved—a series of fish made from coconut shells polished to a high sheen and attached by leather straps to swim around his waist. This sad souvenir was passed on to my mother but upon *her* passing was not found among any of her possessions.

Frozen at the Altar

The actual exchanges during the perpetual confrontations between him and my mother have been erased from my consciousness, except for two particular incidents that remain as clear as the warning against eating poisonous piles of paint flakes.

One is of waking up from a nap on the bottom bunk in the room I shared with my sister to find my mother curled around me, bending me to her fetal position, and sobbing into my tiny shoulder. Timidly, I asked her what was wrong. "Bob…Bobby yy-yelled at me," was her wet, pathetic response. How lonely, how despairing was this confession. What pain and helplessness poured forth through those four gasping words. I was glued to the sheets by my mother's tears, paralyzed with uncertainty and impotence. What was expected of me? How could I rescue my mother? These two questions became my unhappy inheritance, endowed by untrustworthy executors, the very same who were charged with my care and protection.

The other remembrance finds my mother on her knees in front of our freezer, with its pull-out drawer on the bottom of the refrigerator. As she unpacked groceries she cried in front of this sub-zero altar while my uncle, standing over her, acted the merciless Inquisitor. Thundering accusations were his sermon and pitiful tears were her penance, offered for perceived assaults on Bobby's sensibilities, and being stored away—frozen foods and memories to be defrosted at some undetermined future time. I, the unwilling congregant, understood this rite as little as I did the Latin spoken by our priest during Sunday mass. *Mea culpa, mea culpa, mea maxima culpa.* One need not speak a dusty language to understand the vernacular of guilt and fear and shame.

At some point one of Bobby's dates morphed from a one-night fling into a more permanent arrangement and he moved out. I didn't wake up to the smell of frying steak anymore, and the shouting between him and my mother came to an end, but in some intangible way he was never completely gone. Threat and fear aren't cleared out as easily as the stench of fried steak and motorcycle oil.

Miss Evelyn and a Port Wine Stain

My mother was a graduate of Hunter College and became an early childhood educator. She secured a teaching position in an elementary school further out on Long Island, in Suffolk County. My sister Paula used to call it "Suffer County." Being a denizen of the City, my mother had never needed a driver's license. Therefore, we all woke early in order for my mother to endure her daily trek by bus, train, and taxi to that mystical place called Manetuck Elementary School in West Islip, an all-white enclave of learning that was baptized with a Native American appellation in honor of a tribe that no longer existed. My sister and I, meanwhile, endured the hospitality and semi-vigilant eye of Miss Evelyn, the neighborhood babysitter.

My mother's high school graduation picture.

Miss Evelyn had three children of her own: a girl of 15 named Trudy (a truly striking name to my ears), a boy named Butch (to whom I had secretly given my heart), and a younger daughter whose name escapes me. There was an assortment of neighborhood children at Miss Evelyn's, of varying ages and sex, but Paula and I were singular in that we were the only white children, a fact that didn't impact my consciousness until I was a teenager.

Getting up and out before the morning's light was a strain on all of us, compounded when I cried to my mother that I couldn't eat breakfast at Miss Evelyn's; the whites of her eggs were runny and made me gag. So we got up even earlier for my mother to make us the kind of eggs to which we were accustomed—cheerful golden mounds surrounded by perfectly cooked whites fried in real butter, not margarine, and freckled with black pepper.

Off we trudged then to Miss Evelyn's, where my day was spent in a blur of black-and-white cartoons, half-day kindergarten, and waiting for Mommy to get back home, at which time we retraced our steps in the waning light of day, back to our private jungle in the city. There weren't many events that distinguished one day from the rest, just a few fleeting ones, so that when I recall my early youth it seems as if my years of being four and five actually transpired over the scant few days of which I have memory.

Bedstands and Barstools

Two disquieting recollections involve Miss Evelyn's husband. Given that we were never, to my knowledge, formally introduced, I thought of him as Mr. Evelyn. That breach of formality, however, did not hinder him from enticing me into his bedroom. Was he home sick from work? Unemployed? Sleeping off a drunk? I'll never know. But I do know that he was in bed, in a darkened room, and I too was in the bed, close enough to see the port wine stain that covered the lower right half of his face. Why was I in the bedroom of this nameless, soulless man, and why was I so close to this stranger's face, and where was Miss Evelyn? Lucky children meet their coaches on green, sunny fields—men who encourage their charges to run to base or make a goal; mine was lying in a dark bedroom, slyly encouraging me to creep farther up the bed toward his pillow.

A seemingly happier experience with Mr. Evelyn does come to mind, one that took place in sunny daylight—at least initially. Mr. Evelyn and I were, for some reason, walking together on one of the broad sidewalks of Queens. The sun was so bright it dimmed all the neon signs in its path. We stepped from the blinding white daylight into the smoky gray of what I now know was a neighborhood bar.

Mr. Evelyn was quite jovial that day, and I heard many hearty replies to his raucous greeting. Once my eyes adjusted I saw a shiny, if nicked, wooden counter with stools lined up in front. Mr. Evelyn hoisted me up on one—a wobbly affair with sticky red vinyl to cover the seat—and was kind enough to share his bitter, foamy drink. I don't remember getting down from the stool, or leaving the acrid smelling bar, or getting back to Miss Evelyn's.

The experience is one of those that is a mental flash freeze; it has a definite timeframe but isn't connected to anything preceding or following, yet it buzzes in my mind like an annoying gnat. Thinking back on this incident raises questions in my mind: Why did Mr. Evelyn choose *me* to go with him that day? Did he take other children on other days? Why would a grown man even be interested in having a girl, barely out of toddlerhood, accompany him to a bar and share his beer? The questions are painful to consider, and painful even to *have* to consider. And most painful of all, they are questions that will never have answers.

One day Miss Evelyn put out cookies and a fancy china dish filled with some kind of food I had never seen before. Little polished wooden beads were piled up in the bowl, like an unchained rosary. Why anyone would want to eat them was beyond me. My interest was further piqued when Miss Evelyn gave a stern warning to us children to stay out of them. Of course this only intensified my curiosity—now I wondered what they tasted like as well!

I tried to be obedient. I stole surreptitious peeks at the dish, which was displayed on an occasional table near the living room window. A shaft of sunlight beamed right on that dish, a spotlight of temptation that called me, beckoned me. It was a veritable halo of palpable, pulsating enticement.

My resistance finally abandoned me. I crossed the threshold into the room. Consequences conveniently out of mind, I plunged my fingers in the dish, grabbed a few of the oily beads, and popped them in my mouth. They were salty, and smooth on my tongue. I rolled them around in my mouth, hearing them click against my teeth before biting down. Cautiously I crunched one. Why, they tasted like the peanut butter Miss Evelyn spread on our sandwiches! How did these crunchy beads become that smooth paste in the jar?

So absorbed was I in contemplating this matter that I never heard Miss Evelyn approach until she was right in front of me. She looked down at me, arms akimbo, eyes narrowed and blazing. I stood frozen to the floor. My face, I hoped, conveyed nothing but innocence. The peanut-y taste was replaced by the electric tingling of fear.

Looming over me she demanded, "Were you eatin' mah peanuts?"

With eyes as big and round as the bowl that held those sinful nuts, eyes that desperately pleaded my false virtue, I shook my head.

She was not to be so easily convinced. "Open yo' mouth," Miss Evelyn commanded.

Slowly, I complied. Bits of semi-chewed peanuts condemned me as they hung from my teeth and shone on my tongue. She peered into my mouth. Without a word she straightened up, drew back her arm, and gave one hard slap to my cheek. She pointed to the doorway and followed me as I slunk out of the room.

I tried to absorb what had happened. My cheek burned. The peanuts stuck in my dry throat. I was too shocked to cry; no one had ever hit me like that. Surely eating a few peanuts couldn't be such an offense as to warrant that hateful strike. Apparently, snack foods were strictly for adults and I had unwittingly violated some unwritten culinary code.

That cruel incident has remained with me, and now I understand that Miss Evelyn was only a frustrated woman with a houseful of kids and a lazy drunk of a husband. All the same, whenever I eat cocktail peanuts I do get a certain sense of vindication.

God's Name is Spot

Miss Evelyn escorted me to and from school. My memories of primary school are as spotty as most children's, but the red and blue book bag I proudly carried back and forth sticks firmly in my mind. I had picked it out from all the others after long and careful consideration in front of the "Back to School" display on the second floor of Woolworth's. It was the perfect size and shape to accommodate my new No. 2 pencils and pink Sharpie eraser, as well as my black and white marbled notebook.

Miss Starr was my teacher, and never was one more aptly named. If the artists at Disney Studio had been commissioned to create the ideal teacher, Miss Starr would have flowed effortlessly from their pens. She had brown wavy hair, and wore soft flowery dresses, and never, ever raised her voice. Her complexion was smooth and always set in a pleasant expression. I'm fairly certain no tempera jungle besmirched the walls of her home, and peanuts were there for the taking.

Miss Starr used one of those universal tools of the elementary schoolteacher: the multi-pronged chalk holder. I loved the smell of chalk and the slight rasping sound it made on the slate. I loved how it was white, yet translucent at the same time. I loved how curls and lines and angles made words that meant something. This was like another world, with its own smells and sounds and images and codes, and I was allowed to enter freely and roam and explore.

Miss Starr drew perfectly parallel lines on the board in which she wrote short sentences formed in big block letters. I was enormously proud of the fact that I read better than most in my class. My mother had taught me when I was four. In spite of overwhelming shyness I sometimes volunteered to read what Miss Starr had written. It wasn't about showing off—it was just that when I saw those beautiful letters, so white against the ebony of the blackboard, I was compelled to read them. The words had the power to draw me out of myself and permit me to perform something I never would attempt on my own.

One day Miss Starr wrote some sentences and asked for a volunteer to read them. I raised my hand and was selected. Quietly but confidently I read, "My god's name is Spot."

Why were all the other kids laughing? I looked with confusion at Miss Starr's benignly smiling face.

My gaze returned to the board and I silently worded the sentence to myself, this time to read correctly, "My *dog's* name is Spot." With blazing red cheeks and a churning in my stomach I realized I had unwittingly christened the Supreme Being as "Spot," not the canine being Miss Starr had intended. I felt my face and ears get as hot as if the Almighty was already condemning me for my unintended blasphemy.

I don't remember ever again volunteering in that class for anything. Maybe I did, but the point is that I was already forged into a person unable to overcome even the smallest, most inconsequential error. Some other child—one who enjoyed being accepted for who she was and not for how she performed—might blithely shrug the whole thing off and maybe reward the loudest laugher in the class with a good kick on the recess field. I, however, was not able to get past the feelings of shame and inadequacy and inferiority. I think this was the first time, and therefore the keystone, of my feeling of always being outside the group and an object of ridicule. Painfully shy to begin with, it only took one incident like this to cause me to further draw into myself.

Become insulated. Stay safe. Don't invite attention.

This is how I operated for years afterward. But where does a five-year-old learn such intense, crippling self-doubt and recrimination? I'm pretty sure it had something to do with a chronically depressed mother, an uncle of uncontrolled passions, and a man of decidedly questionable morals whose face was scarred with a port-wine stain.

We Gotta Get Outta This Place

One evening we had an unforgettable trip home from Miss Evelyn's. My mother, Paula, and I traipsed through the chill and waning daylight of autumn. As we arrived at the last street to cross before reaching our apartment a mob blocked our way.

Policemen took position on the street corners. Onlookers strained their necks to see over the crowd.

We learned that a teenage boy had come home to find his parents embroiled in a fight of unequal advantages. He decided to even the odds by grabbing the largest knife in the house and stabbing his father multiple times. Upon the older man's near demise, and the impending arrival of the law, he ran from the house and hid out somewhere in the vicinity.

The police eventually apprehended him and allowed the assemblage to continue on our respective paths. I was not reassured. My heart pounded so hard that my ribs rattled. I tripped clumsily over the broken pavement of the sidewalk. The climb up that long, dark staircase to our apartment seemed ominous and full of the peril that surely would manifest itself as soon as we opened the door. Without a doubt, each step brought us closer to this homicidal adolescent who was lurking in our apartment and waiting for us, his next victims.

The fact that he had been caught was inconsequential; my imagination and fear were stronger than the police.

Years later, when recounting our move from Queens, my mother played out the scenario she attributed to our moving. She turned our move from Queens to the gentler (and supposedly safer) locale of the suburbs—the aforementioned Suffolk County on Long Island—into a joke. "Yes," she set the stage for her punch line, "I knew it was time to move when Ellen wanted a nickel and asked me, 'Mammy, can Ah ha' fi' cent?'" It made for a great little anecdote at the time, but I believe the real reason was a combination of unbearably early mornings, dry cleaner fumes, dubious day care, and murderous teenage boys.

I Dream of Jennie

One truly happy memory I have from that time is of my friend Jennie. She lived on the next block with her parents, who had emigrated from the deprivation of China and now owned a laundry in the Promised Land of milk and detergent.

Their apartment was in the back of the business and smelled wonderful. The combination of steam from the washers and whatever was cooking in the perpetually bubbling cast iron pot made for a starchy, exotic scent. Jennie's parents didn't speak English, apart from laundry-lingo, and each sported several prominent gold teeth. But none of that mattered to me; they were gracious enough to teach a five-year-old left-handed white girl how to eat with chopsticks.

I was so enamored of this family that when we were comfortably ensconced in the Land of the White People (Suffolk County) and I received as a gift a lovely blonde doll, I named her Jennie. I kept her long enough to eventually (and somewhat reluctantly) relinquish her care to my own daughter.

I wish there was more to write about Jennie and her parents because they were an important part of my life at that time. I always felt happy when I was at their home, and for all I know it was only a handful of times. If I'm left with a dearth of memories about this loving family, ultimately that's OK because I have a warm place in my heart when I think of them, and in the end, that's all that matters.

Show Me the Money

Occasionally, our landlord, the owner of the dry cleaners downstairs, had errands to run and in a pinch my mother stepped in to mind the store. Sometimes I was allowed to accompany her and had the privilege of sitting on top of the counter and "helping."

My favorite thing to do was to work the register. It was an intricate, complicated machine, with brass curlicues and round keys overlaid with ivory that undoubtedly had been involuntarily donated by some poor slaughtered behemoth of Asia or Africa.

I pressed my finger onto the yellowed ivory and watched as numbered tin tabs magically popped up in the window. The transaction was completed by pushing hard on the biggest button. *Bang!* The drawer opened with a fanfare, revealing its treasure of shiny, jingling coins and crinkled bills. I studied the contents of each curved compartment and dropped the customers' coins into the appropriate bins. Triumphantly I pushed the drawer shut with as much flourish as can be expected from a cashier in kindergarten.

Put on a Happy Face

Being denizens of the City, we walked everywhere when possible, whatever the weather. On this particular occasion, a gray cloudy day, the three of us were strolling down the sidewalk. Mommy was in the middle with Paula on one side and me on the other. We were all holding hands. We passed a store window and I saw a doll. Not too big, not too small, just right for me to hold.

Me in the "happy face" hat.

"Mommy, look at that pretty doll! Can we buy it?" I asked excitedly.

"No," Mommy said brusquely.

"Please? She is just so pretty," I implored.

"I said *no*. Now keep walking," Mommy ordered.

I looked up at her, the last vestige of hope fading away as I saw the ever-present frown on her forehead deepen. I mimicked her face unintentionally and felt my own forehead furrow.

"Don't you look at me like that," Mommy reprimanded. "What's with that ugly face? Walk in front of me so I can see the happy face on your hat."

I was wearing a green cable-knit hat with a furry white border that embellished the back, and which tied under my chin. Knitted into the back of the hat was a face—two bright eyes, a pert little nose, and two red smiling lips.

"I'd rather see that hat than your face."

So Mommy thought my face was ugly and didn't want to hold my hand anymore. A cloud fell from the sky and crawled across my heart.

The Cure Could Kill You

Only once did I see our landlord outside of his store. I was sitting on top of a stool. Paula was seated on the floor. My mother was standing in front of me, determinedly clutching a brown glass bottle in one hand and a spoon in the other. I don't remember if the bottle contained Geritol, fish oil, or some other godawful concoction that was inflicted on children in those days. The misguided conviction was It's Healthy For Them.

Regardless, I was making a fuss over taking it. Apparently it was a *loud* fuss. And on top of that, my distress had transferred itself to Paula, so we were both howling and wailing like orphaned puppies. To add to the commotion, my mother shouted at us, insisting that this was *good for you* and I had better *open up and swallow it*.

We must have been at barrier-breaking decibel levels because all of a sudden our landlord exploded through the door like the cavalry at Little Big Horn. Simultaneously, he asked *what in the hell is going on* but of course he had to shout to be heard over the three of us. The ensuing Sturm und Drang must have sounded like we were performing a quartet from the grand finale of a Wagnerian opera.

When he found out this was all over a spoonful of "medicine," Mr. Dry Cleaner sarcastically suggested that the cure, indeed, was worse than the condition it was supposed to remedy. He clomped back down the stairs, emphatically slamming the door for a final flourish.

The Bus Ride that Wasn't

As previously mentioned, I was a good reader and loved reading. My mother saw to it that we girls had access to all manner of books—

children's poetry, fairy tales, story books… one of which was *Little Black Sambo*, the story of a dark-skinned East Indian boy. This was a truly great story in my mind because it involved pancakes and butter.

After a day of shopping we waited at the bus stop for our ride home. When it arrived, I climbed the three rubber-covered steps, Paula trailing behind, as my mother deposited the fare into the coin box. I looked to the seating area which was pretty full, mostly of black people.

"Mommy!" I exclaimed in excitement. "Look at all the black Sambos!"

Sputtering, gasping, my mother grabbed each of us girls by the hand, turned, and dragged us off the bus, lost fare be damned.

The fare wasn't the only thing lost, apparently.

Only a few years ago did I learn that without telling anyone in the family, my mother had moved us surreptitiously from Manhattan to Queens. The three of us were AWOL. One day we were in an apartment on Carmine Street and the next we were gone. My grandfather hired a private detective who somehow tracked us to the apartment over the dry cleaners. I'm sure the eventual reunion was not pleasant. In an attempt to further distance herself from her parents she decided we were to leave the City and find more congenial environs.

Silver, Not Gold

My mother supplemented her income by teaching over the summer breaks at Creative Day Camp in Valley Stream, which was predominantly for Jewish kids. Paula and I got to go for free. A guy named Eddie Silver owned it, and he was a one of a kind character. He kept dog biscuits for treats in his pocket and I remember when we drove to camp with him several times he charged down the road singing "Boola Boola" at the top of his lungs. Creative was the perfect name for his camp, as there was a heavy emphasis on art. I really liked Eddie, and I liked his daughter, Brenda. I know he liked us too because he visited our apartment several times…

Eddie came over and immediately the ambiance in our apartment became sunny and charged with energy. Eddie was quite the charismatic fellow. My mother liked him. A lot. They disappeared into my mother's room and Paula and I were strictly instructed not to open the door. *Why not?* I wondered. *Was there a problem? Were they playing a game?* Probably; Eddie was so much fun. *I want to play too!* I thought. I'll just take a quick peek… I opened the door and my mother and Eddie were laying on her bed. They were very close to each other. My mother leaped up. "What are you doing?! I told you not to open the door!" I slammed the door shut, confused and scared. I don't remember Eddie coming over after that.

There were several other locations for Creative Day Camps on the Island, and years later Eddie planned on opening one in Puerto Rico. He contacted my mother about being the director; she considered it briefly but ultimately decided to decline the offer. Too bad, that might have been a real adventure.

Here's to You, Miss Evelyn

Subsequently, the summer after first grade my mother found a house to rent farther out on the Island, in West Islip. (Queens is on Long Island but is one of the five boroughs of New York City, so isn't really counted as being part of the Island.) I had an ache in my heart at the thought of leaving Jennie, and I missed Miss Evelyn terribly. For a long time, whenever we were in a crowd I searched all the black faces for her, but I never did find her. The Peanut Incident notwithstanding, I had spent most of my days with her and she was like a second mother. My memories of her are imbued with deep fondness.

Long Island

West Islip

Van Buren—Not the President

We moved into a rental house on Van Buren Avenue in West Islip, two blocks away from Manetuck Elementary, where my mother taught. Paula attended kindergarten and I was in second grade. To put it mildly, I thought we had landed in another universe.

The streets were clean—and quiet! Homes were surrounded by carpets of lush, green lawn instead of dust, gravel, and sidewalks strewn with garbage. There were trees. Not scraggly, exhaust-choked ones, but leafy bowers that towered to the heavens. No buses smoked or rumbled down the roads, and no planes crisscrossed the sky. I was enchanted.

Our house had a driveway and a carport, which was superfluous since not only did we not own a car, but my mother didn't know how to drive. It boasted both a front door and a side door which were on street level—no dark, malevolent stairs to climb. Unbelievably, every room had windows, placed high up on the walls! Stretched out on my bed, as I looked up I saw nothing but blue instead of an alley shaft entombed by blackened brick.

Funny enough, I don't remember if Paula and I had our own rooms. I guess because the house was so bright and spacious, it was large enough to seem like we each had our own domain.

The layout fascinated me. It was a one-story rancher yet the room accessed by the side door was sunken, meaning there were two steps to reach the main living quarters. The idea of rooms on different levels was novel and I felt like I was living in a fairy tale castle. There was even a wrought iron railing from which I swung and looked down into the common room. Pure magic.

The house came equipped with a washer, the kind that had two rollers and a crank handle to squeeze water out of the clothes. It was in the basement. And this is where the aura of sunshine and hope and promise became tarnished.

The Cloud Without a Silver Lining

Our landlady had moved out because of a horrible incident. As my mother recounted to Paula and me, in hushed and reverent voice, this woman's son was a budding musician and played in a marching band. One day after a rehearsal he came home to perform his final piece in life, a solemn, sorrowful solo… In full band regalia he ceremoniously descended to the basement, where he hanged himself.

This tragedy brought our new home out from the clouds in my imagination and landed it squarely back in reality.

On reflection, the mystery is not why the suicide occurred, but why my mother felt compelled to share this information with her daughters, who were only seven and five at the time. Did we really need to know this? Of course not. But my mother's fascination with all things dark and dismal drove her to impart that outlook of the world to us.

Onion Soup

My grandmother—whom everyone referred to as "Mom"—was 100 percent Italian, but uncharacteristic of that ethnicity, did not like onions or garlic. When my grandparents came from the City to visit, my mother made boxed Lipton's onion soup as an appetizer.

"Mom doesn't like onions," I reminded my mother.

"She'll never notice them," Mommy replied with feigned innocence.

I looked into the pot of brown broth, loaded with swirling bits of chopped onions. *How will she not notice?* I wondered.

When it was time to sit down to eat, the pot was put on the table and my mother ladled soup into each bowl. She passed them around. Mom looked at hers in disgust and pushed it aside.

I held my breath.

"Why aren't you eating your soup?" my mother asked.

"It's loaded with onions," Mom replied. "You know I don't like onions."

"There are hardly any in there and the soup has more of a beef flavor from the broth," my mother answered peevishly.

"What are you talking about?" Mom responded, just a little louder. "They're in every spoonful!"

"You are exaggerating! You're just trying to start something! Nothing I ever cook is good enough for you!"

The volleys went back and forth across the table. Tears ensued on both sides. Our soup got cold and a congealed cloud formed over everyone's bowls. My step-grandfather, referred to as Morris, joined the fracas and now it was a three-way fight. The meal was ruined.

When my grandparents were ready to go, Morris, as was his custom, slipped a dollar each to Paula and me.

"That's for ice cream," he told us.

Feeling the lump in my throat, I wasn't sure I'd be able to swallow anything ever again.

Another Time, Another Jungle

For someone who grew up exclusively in New York City, my mother had an amazing talent to create a beautiful garden. If she threw gravel on the ground I believe flowers would flourish. Gardening became her lifelong passion. As scholars pore over ancient scrolls, my mother studied bulb catalogs. As archeologists tediously scrape through layers of soil, my mother dug precisely sized holes in which to gently insert seeds and bulbs.

This talent was not restricted to the outdoors. Every window, shelf, and flat surface was eventually festooned with plants. Her particular favorite was African violets. Vines of pothos became living wallpaper. As if fulfilling a long-ago promise, the painted jungle of our old apartment was exchanged for vibrant, emerald plants that spoke of life and hope, gradually replacing the dark cloud of death that hung over the house.

Words that Hurt

Across the street, up a short, pine-tree shaded driveway, lived the DeCristo family. They had a daughter, Cathy, who was about my age. One cloudless day, in deciding who should be "It," Cathy, the self-appointed leader of our group, started to point and recite the age-old eeny-meeny-miney-moe ditty, but instead of saying "catch a *tiger* by the toe," she said *"nigger."* I was shocked! That was not a word that was used in my family, and my tiny breast swelled with full-blown outrage. I thought of Miss Evelyn, and Butch, and Trudy, and my classmates from Queens. These were people I knew and loved, and I was ashamed to be in the company of someone who thought of them in that term.

I ran into the house and told my mother. She came out and calmly explained to Cathy how that particular word was hurtful and wrong, and shouldn't be used. Mommy went back to the house and we continued with our game. I am happy to say I never heard Cathy use that word again.

On a summer Saturday, as a few of us were playing, the next door neighbor girl, Bernadette, came outside. If possible, she was even more shy than me. She wore very thick glasses — the kind that distort the eyes. Cathy stage-whispered, "My mother says Bernadette's dad beat her mom when she was pregnant, and that's why she has to wear those goofy glasses."

Timid and uncertain, Bernadette approached us. Cathy started sing-songing, "Blind-y Bernadette, blind-y Bernadette." Bernadette immediately burst into tears and ran into her house. Her mother materialized and somehow, other mothers appeared. My mother was furious! I hadn't joined in that heinous choir, but I hadn't walked away, either. I was made to apologize and then was sent to my room. All these years later, I can still remember the hurt on Bernadette's face and the shame I felt.

I hope she went on to have a happier life.

We're Gonna Be Loaded!

Cathy and I were talking about how we'd like to have some money. She came up with a terrific plan—bottle and sell perfume! Imagine, there was a fortune to be made from the ladies in our neighborhood! Luckily for us, Cathy's mother had a garden—a very prolific *rose* garden.

First order of business? Collect the petals to extract their scent. We proceeded to denude every single bush. What a haul! Step two, fill a pot with water—and not just any pot, but the big sauce pot. We needed to make a lot of perfume if we were to rake in the dough. Step number three, put all the rose petals in the pot. Surely once the water started boiling, they would release all their scent, and voila! We'd have gallons of rose perfume.

Sadly, we never got that far. Cathy's mother came home and… well, I'm sure I was sent packing across the street in record time. And Cathy? Well, poor Cathy. The fallout must have been so traumatic that unlike my mother, who thrived on recounting the unsavory elements of life, she knew to put a lid on this pot.

The Tank

I mentioned previously that my mother had never learned to drive. That was about to be rectified; she hired an instructor and took lessons. The big day arrived when she was to take her road test and, as we had hoped, she passed.

Now that she had a license, the logical next step was to acquire a car. She found one—an enormous, hulking tank of a Buick that she immediately had painted a shiny maroon. Whomever she found to do the deed, however, must have had precious little experience, or talent, because the finished product was full of sandy bumps, like automotive acne. Never mind; the car ran and offered us the thrilling anticipation of unexplored highways and back roads.

The evening the painters returned the car, my mother decided to take it for a little spin. She settled herself into the driver's seat, inserted the key, pulled the choke, and... nothing. She tapped slightly on the pedal and gave it a little more gas. Pulled the choke... nothing. She was confused. She did exactly everything she had done before, but now the car didn't start. Not a cough, not a sputter! Disheartened (but not defeated!) she decided to wait until the next day and get some help.

The following morning she called on Mr. DeCristo to check things out. He came over and she showed him exactly what she had done the night before. She settled in the driver's seat. She inserted the key. She pulled out the choke. And that's when Mr. DeCristo roared with laughter. Through his howls he explained she hadn't been pulling out the choke. She'd been engaging the air vent knob.

Boston Bound

My mother was uncharacteristically nervous about driving, whereas her normal modus operandi was to approach tasks with unrestrained enthusiasm, determination, and confidence. Consequently she decided to overcome this apprehension by embarking on a trip—one to test her mettle and result in her being a secure driver. She chose Boston as an optimal destination. Not too far of a drive, to be concluded with a triumphant entry into the city, sailing across Cape Cod Bay in a ferry.

At long last The Day arrived. Bags were packed, snacks were in hand, and the cat was fostered. The first challenge was to get off the Island, which meant going over a bridge, navigating converging lanes at a toll booth, and not missing the turnoff for the New England Thruway. Mommy aced it. We were as excited as pioneers hacking their way to the New West.

Not too long into the adventure, however, the tedium of the trip took hold, as did discomfort. Previous to our departure to points north, the seats in the car were outfitted with plastic covers. They were clear and covered with little pockets—air cushions, presumably—which made the traveler's experience not unlike sitting on bubble wrap. They were highly effective in keeping the seats clean, but caused the unhappy passenger to soon be ensconced in a puddle of sweat.

All the windows were rolled down, so the exhaust from every passing vehicle—tractor trailers included—perfumed the interior. I became car sick in no time flat. Once we reached less crowded roadways, however, the motion sickness wore off and my sister and I played alphabet games using license plates and billboards and road signs to find letters. (License plates were great when you needed a "Z," "X," or "Q"). "A my name is..." "I went on a picnic and in my basket I put..." and so many others. My mother drilled us on math problems. She whistled tunes and we had to guess what the song was. We sang out loud. We counted railroad cars as trains went by. In short, before we knew it we were in Massachusetts!

My mother found her way to the docks and my sister and I watched in amazement as our car disappeared into the belly of the ferry. As we waited our turn to board, the sky ominously turned gray. This was not a good sign. Once on board we found a spot on wooden benches and waved to people on shore. The ship gave a mournful blast of its horn, backed out of the slip, and started a slow turn to face the water head on.

The sky got grayer.

The water got choppier.

And I got sicker.

Being car sick was nothing compared to this! Every slap of a wave caused me to become queasier. I closed my eyes. No! That made it worse. I tried looking for our destination but all I saw was the horizon going up and down, up and down, up and… I could hold it in no longer. I threw up overboard, and not alone, I might add. There was some small comfort in the fact that I wasn't the only one with seasickness, and the others were even grownups, including a group of habit-clad nuns.

Eventually, thankfully, we arrived at our destination. We disembarked and to my amazement when my feet hit terra firma I felt better. We retrieved our car and drove to the hotel where we had reservations for the night. When we got to our room, in addition to a vase of fresh flowers, we found a fruit basket to welcome us. We never found out who sent the fruit, but whoever our benefactor was, we were pleased and thankful. That night we slept on soft beds, the air lightly scented with the perfume of roses and Asian lilies. Sweaty seat covers of the "tank" and choking exhaust of passing vehicles seemed like just a bad dream.

Long Island

North Babylon

It's All Ours

After a year in West Islip my mother found a house to buy in the nearby town of North Babylon — our renting days were over. It was an adorable Cape Cod with a huge maple tree in the front and a nice long backyard in which my mother indulged her passion for gardening. Bordering our backyard were woods that made a barrier between all the neighborhood houses and muffled the sounds of Sunrise Highway.

The house was small but cozy, precisely the right size for our little family of three. There was a living room, kitchen, bathroom, and two bedrooms on the first floor, a finished attic consisting of two rooms, and an unfinished basement with an untarnished history. Paula and I shared the one bedroom and my mother had the other. We had very nice neighbors on either side, and a family of Italians across the street who owned three houses in a row. An elderly couple named the Dieterles lived on the right. Mr. and Mrs. Sabatini lived with their son Frank on the left. My mother worked two jobs and Frank became our babysitter when she needed to be out in the evening.

Baubles, Bangles, and Beads

One moonlighting job Mommy had was selling Sarah Coventry jewelry. She paid for a sample kit which, in addition to the items of jewelry, included a zippered pouch to hold catalogs, order forms, and pens. Might a young girl wish for anything better to peruse? Pins, bracelets, necklaces, earrings, some with stones, some with "gems." Others were unadorned, but the gold and silver sparkled nonetheless. There was a black velvet cloth on which to display the merchandise, and which showed them off to their best advantage. My absolute favorite was a pin called "Song of India." This conjured up all kinds of romantic, exotic images. Peacocks. The Taj Mahal.

Multi-colored, bright saris. Sitar music. Fantasies in which an imaginative girl could get lost.

A new necklace was introduced to the line and my mother bought one for her kit. Its big selling point was that it was unbreakable. My mother included it in her next booking. I heard her recount the experience to a friend: "I told the ladies this necklace was virtually indestructible. Toddlers could yank on it. It could get caught on a hanger. Anything! All with no harm done. I proceeded to demonstrate. I held one end in each hand and gave it a yank. The damn thing broke and beads went flying everywhere." Needless to say, it was not a big seller that night.

Ironically, my mother never wore jewelry. No rings. Her ears hadn't been pierced and she didn't see the sense in painful clip-ons. Not even a watch! Why she decided to pick this particular line as an income supplement is beyond me. But I had fun while it lasted, and she got some pretty good anecdotes out of it.

Fun for Free

We lived in North Babylon, at 92 Liberty Avenue, but Mommy still taught at Manetuck Elementary. Around this time the estimated average salary for an elementary school teacher was $6,800; adjusted for inflation that was worth a little over $54,000 in 2020. Our house had cost $17,000 (my mother paid a whopping $500 as a downpayment!) and mortgage interest rates averaged 5 percent. But we never seemed to have any money. Therefore, much of our entertainment involved free outings.

One of my mother's favorite pastimes was to tour model homes of the planned communities springing up all over the Island. She just could not get over the size of the closets. "You could rent one out to a family of Puerto Ricans," was her assessment. Tromping through the woods was her idea of a great time—spotting different kinds of birds and identifying wildflowers. We carried a big goldfish bowl on our foray into the (relative) wild and she demonstrated how to make a terrarium. And, of course, there was the library.

Eating out, Paula and I were trained to look at the right-hand side of the menu, where the prices were listed, and to select our meal based on that. The amount of groceries purchased was predicated on how much money was in Mommy's wallet. We often walked to the grocery store and trudged home carrying paper bags of goods. I really hated this, not because of the distance walked, or the number of bags carried, but because my socks always slid down in my shoes.

Another deficit was in our wardrobes. I sometimes got new clothing, but Paula wore many of my outgrown clothes. Happily, relief came in the form of a fellow teacher of my mother's.

Mommy had made friends with a lovely woman named Sarita Lamm. She was a short, round lady with very black hair and very black-rimmed glasses. But so sweet! Her name did her justice. She had a daughter who was a year older than me, which was a happy circumstance because I received bags of clothing that her daughter outgrew. They had very good taste, and several of the dresses gifted to me became favorites. The best one was butter yellow with short sleeves and a wide skirt. It was overlaid with white dotted Swiss. An embellishment of pink roses crossed the bodice.

My favorite dress, yellow and white dotted Swiss with roses, a gift from Mrs. Lamm.

Mrs. Lamm, I wish you could have known how happy you made me.

Rice and Coffee

Paula and I were on our own a good bit — in those days it was safe to leave children unattended for a while. Much of that time occurred after school because we got home before our mother. This is when I started experimenting with cooking… sometimes with good results.

One afternoon I decided to make rice with butter and cheese. Since my mother didn't like potatoes we ate rice a lot, and loved it. I knew how to season the rice (butter, grated cheese, salt and pepper) but what I didn't know was how to cook it. Not realizing that rice expands during cooking I dumped what looked like enough rice for the two of us in the pot.

In 10 minutes there was a virtual volcano of bubbling white. A vision of my mother's disembodied angry face floated before my mind's eye. To avert almost certain punishment I told Paula we had to eat it all. My mother couldn't understand why neither one of us was hungry for supper that night.

Rice in its many incarnations — with butter and cheese, with sugar and cinnamon and milk for breakfast, fried in the Chinese fashion — was delicious to me. But the day my mother brought home groceries that included a brand new rice product, a whole different world opened up. I had seen it advertised on TV and here it was in our very own home. Rice-a-Roni, the San Francisco treat! This rectangular box held all the ingredients for a truly exceptional delight — rice, vermicelli (I didn't know what that was but it sounded foreign and that was what was important), pilaf, and a packet of secret spices! I felt positively regal as I ate dinner that night, food on my plate that came all the way from the Golden State.

Paula and I looked forward to a snack after school and I declared myself in charge. Gearing up to make something sweet, I retrieved my mother's giant recipe book (stiff olive green covers with yellowed, stained pages) and found one for a coffee marble cake. *Hey, Mommy loves coffee. She will really enjoy this!* The only problem was that the recipe called for brewed coffee and I didn't know how to use the stove-top percolator. I came up with an inspired solution.

Instead of putting liquid coffee in the recipe I mixed grounds in the batter. *This will be wonderful,* I thought—just like chocolate chips, the grounds would melt during baking and make delicious little bursts of coffee flavor throughout the cake.

This is when I learned that coffee grounds do not melt.

The result was a cake that was as gritty as the sands of Jones Beach. Thankfully, my mother wasn't mad and without a word of reproach, and I suspect with a chuckle, tossed the whole cake in the garbage.

Chinese Red

When my mother decided to paint the living room I begged her to let me help, but to no avail. Oh, how I wanted to paint! So... one afternoon after school I decided I absolutely was going to do exactly that.

Hmm... what to paint? I know! My closet. I could paint the inside of my closet and my mother need never see it and therefore never know. Now, to pick a color. I went down to the basement where there was a rainbow of paint cans to choose from. One was labeled "Chinese Red." Beautiful!

Can and brush in hand, I went up to my bedroom and got to work. To achieve maximum efficiency, and to lessen the amount of labor, I left all of our clothes in the closet. I pried off the paint can lid and marveled not only at the deep, rich color, but also at the sheen. This was because, unbeknownst to me, this wasn't paint; this was enamel.

Oh, our closet was going to look absolutely majestic. I was sure no Oriental palace ever looked any more exotic than my own secret Chinese closet. I dipped the tool in the can and enthusiastically put brush to surface. It glided with smooth strokes and the paint went on like liquid velvet. It was glorious. Never mind about the dots of paint getting on our clothes; we could pick them off later when they dried. Oops! Some got on our shoes. That's okay, we could wipe it off afterwards.

Up and down, up and down, the brush did its work. I was mesmerized by the rhythm. Even the fumes were intoxicating. My reverie was broken when Paula, the trusty lookout, rushed into the room to tell me that Mommy was home.

Quick! Cap the can and push it to the back of the closet! Get on the bed and prop up a book to convey innocence and perhaps a touch of ennui.

Mommy walked into the house. No *hello* to us girls. No *how was school?* But instead, a portentous inquiry.

"Who has been painting?"

I immediately shrank from the threatening tone of her voice. How did she know? Did Paula rat me out?

Mommy followed her nose, which led directly to our bedroom. I think she didn't know whether to cry or explode when she saw each and every right shoulder of our clothing adorned with Chinese Red enamel. The Grand Imperial Empress took pity on us, however, and no samurai were summoned.

A Tidal Wave in the Dance Studio

When Paula and I were six and eight, Mommy enrolled us in ballet school. We exulted in our leotards, tutus, and bodices. But for me, the ballet slippers were the best part. They were a blush pink with gray felted soles, and the most unbelievably soft satin on the vamping (top of the slipper). With these on my feet I didn't even need lessons! When I put them on I was transfigured into a lithe, weightless sprite. Of course, sadly, that wasn't the case and I *did* need lessons.

So off we went, Paula and I, to a ballet studio that was already full of little prima donnas and their hopeful mothers. We learned the five foot positions and the basic *port de bras* (arm positions). Enthusiastic students that we were, Paula and I practiced them most seriously.

The weeks of lessons passed by and then the dance instructor (a woman of indefatigable patience, I'm sure) told us little girls that we were going to engage in interpretive dance. As we lined up she gave each of us the choice of a long scarf or a feathered boa from a box. Perhaps she was looking for the next Isadora Duncan.

As we clutched our accoutrements the teacher started a record. I'm almost positive it was Debussy's *La Mer*. Why, you ask? Because we were to interpret the music as waves or mermaids or whatever came to our minds per the sea. As the mothers watched in proud anticipation we held our scarves and boas and began to flutter and twirl and swoop gently to the music.

Except Paula.

Paula rushed past us in a frenzy, waving her scarf like she was bringing in a jet for the landing. As we serenely glided our way around the studio Paula dashed in and out of us, arms flapping, feet galumphing, sweat beads beginning to course down the side of her face. Madame eyed her with consternation. This went on until the needle was lifted off the record.

We returned our scarves and boas to the box, went into the back room and changed into our street clothes. Emerging to find our mothers I noticed that Mommy had edged herself to the back of the room, not part of the parents who were kvelling over their little ballerina darlings. Mommy hustled Paula and me double-time out of the building and into the car.

"Paula!" Mommy exclaimed with exasperation. "You were supposed to be interpreting the music as the sea, like a mermaid or something. Didn't you see what all the other little girls were doing?"

"I did!" Paula replied. "I was the tidal wave!"

Our ballet lessons didn't last very long.

Little Rockefellers

Paula and I had our share of board games, and I loved to play Solitaire, but my favorite game was "bank." Every other Friday my mother waited in a line snaking through the local institution in order to cash her paycheck. Happily, while waiting, Paula and I helped ourselves to handfuls of deposit and withdrawal slips to bring home and add to our "bank."

At some point I had acquired a portable typewriter—a compact, green machine that was Olympic brand, "the Mercedes Benz of typewriters." I set this up on a rickety metal folding table. Our bank slips were assembled in two tidy stacks, along with a row of Monopoly money, in ascending order of denomination. A few pens and freshly sharpened pencils were lined up like legionnaires.

Paula knocked on the bedroom door in her assigned role of a customer in need of a loan. I ushered her in with my call of "Next!" I grilled her on why she needed money. Satisfied, I graciously granted her the loan and she filled out the requisite paper. I typed up the loan on the Olympic and then counted out the money. Sometimes she made a deposit but that wasn't as much fun because there was less paperwork involved (unless I had to make change). We both felt very important and grown up, and the irony wasn't lost on me when years later I worked as a bank teller.

I Will Kill You

Paula was seven years old and, as usual, out playing by herself in the woods. My grandparents had come to visit and it was time to eat. My mother called for Paula to come in but there was no response. Had she snuck in unseen? I was sent to check the attic and basement. My mother went to check outside.

The Dieterles had taken in a border, and I had overheard my mother talking about him. He had recently been released from a mental hospital. (There was a locally famous mental hospital on Long Island called Pilgrim State. We drove past it once and it looked every bit as gothic and foreboding as something in a Dickens or Brontë novel.) We had very strict instructions that we were *never* to be near this man or talk to him.

When Mommy went out to look for Paula, where did she discover her? In the woods with none other than said ex-mental patient. Paula, in all innocence and naiveté, told my mother—as was later recounted—that he was going to "show her some snakes." In short order my mother sent Paula to the house.

With clenched teeth and slitted eyes, she turned to this man. "*You.* You are to stay away from my girls. You may not talk to them. You may not be near them. You may not look at them. If you do, I. Will. Kill. You."

I have no doubt, even to this day, that Mommy meant every word of it. Unhappily for Paula, she got the beating of her life. She screamed at each wallop on her backside. My grandparents knew better than to interfere, so they just sat in their seats and looked nervously down into their plates.

My mother and Paula returned to the table and we commenced our meal, Paula's stifled sobs accompanying each forkful.

Can't Rain (or Snow) on Our Parade

The only times I enjoyed being out of doors was in the winter. We had a good bit of snow in those days, and Paula and I built snowmen, but even better, we constructed igloos! Sledding was a favorite activity, and we would trudge through the woods and climb up the hill that topped out at Deer Park Avenue. Then we gleefully slid down the snowy slope at what we were convinced were supersonic speeds.

Up and down we went until the sun started to sink in the sky. We reluctantly retraced our steps to the house where we shed snowsuits, boots, hats, and mittens—all of which were crusted with snow. Anticipating our return, Mommy already had the oven turned on low for us to prop our feet on the open door to warm ourselves. As we regained feeling in our fingers and toes she served us hot chocolate that she had heated in a pan, whipped with an egg beater to make it frothy. Those were great days.

Indoors was no less entertaining, the attic being a great place for Paula and me to play. Our favorite activity was dress-up. My aunt Wendy had gifted us with some evening gowns she no longer wanted, and which we gratefully received. We selected—with great deliberation and discernment—which dress was appropriate to each scenario we devised.

A favorite and oft-selected one was that we were princesses who had to escape from our evil father, the king. We traipsed between the two rooms of the attic, pretending we were in the forest. Of course all ended happily when we were each rescued by a handsome prince.

The basement was just as much fun. A little table held our Monopoly game. We played it so often that I memorized the order in which to pile the deed cards. I even knew all the rents by heart. We had a lunch bag full of rubber bands to make our Chinese jump rope with. My mother had painted several different hopscotch patterns on the floor, and we were allowed to adorn the walls with our artwork rendered in chalk. Rainy days afforded us unlimited ways to entertain ourselves, whether at the top or the bottom of the house.

Fire and Ice

Fire

Summer in those days felt brutal... unless we were at the beach, which thankfully was quite often. Otherwise, there wasn't much relief from the heat. When Mommy decided we needed a day by the ocean we collected all the paraphernalia—why did it seem to take hours?—and finally made it to the car.

Driving with the windows down offered welcome relief, until we hit the Robert Moses Causeway. Other than the ferry, the Causeway was the only way to get from North Babylon to the beaches. And everybody in the universe—or so it seemed—took this road. Stop and go, stop and go. The sparkling water below the parkway taunted us, the gently lapping waves calling to us like the Sirens of Greek mythology. When would we ever get there?

Of course we did, but our ordeal was far from over.

Unless we were on the sand or in the water, the heat was stifling. The parking lots at both Jones Beach and Fire Island were huge and often necessitated a long walk to our final destination. There was no avoiding it so resignedly we opened the doors of our sweltering car, grabbed our towels, pails, shovels, and flip-flops, and trudged down to the sand.

Walking across the macadam I saw heat waves undulating before me. I smelled the salt from the ocean but it seemed miles away. Gulls cawed and swooped, jeering at us. Sweat beadlets rolled down my spine, making me itch in a place that I couldn't reach to scratch. The sun burned my eyes. (Paula and I didn't have sunglasses.) This was no fun! I'd rather be on my bed with a book!

But then... blessed relief was in sight. As we stepped onto the boardwalk the sparkling carpet of sand spread out before us as far as we could see, and then — hurray! — the ocean. No more waves of heat, but white-capped teal and blue and gray and green waves that rolled endlessly to the shore. Heaven! I inhaled gulps of air laden with the incongruous mix of salt from the water and tar from the parking lot. It was unexplainably enticing. Our energy suddenly renewed, Paula and I were ready to race to the water.

But not so fast!

First we needed to scope out the optimal spot on which to lay our towels. My mother was insistent on this critical maneuver. She scoured the rows of sunbathers, searching for the ideal site, which meant no party that smoked or had a transistor radio (she refused to be subjected to rock and roll, which played on every AM station). Eyes squinting like a general surveying the battlefield, her arm rose up as in a salute and her index finger directed our gaze to the desired location. The race was on!

Our job, Paula's and mine, was to get down to said spot and secure it before anyone beat us to it. Towels flapping, pails and shovels plonking against our legs, we eagerly ran a serpentine pattern around sunbathers, being careful not to trip over chairs or umbrellas. Once relieved of our gear we gratefully sloshed our feet into the blessedly cool ocean.

My mother had a strict rule that we were not to go into the water past our knees. That put a real damper on our fun. The one place I felt anything close to being brave was in the ocean. I loved body surfing. Toes gripping wet compacted sand, balancing unsteadily against incoming waves, I lumbered out as far as allowed and waited for the perfect wave. Flattening my body to a horizontal position I then rode into shore.

There was something about the water that seemed so natural and almost nurturing to me. I felt free and unencumbered. My mind was on neutral. My body gave itself over to the power of the sea. It was a magical, ethereal experience and I emerged like a spirit reborn.

I was not a spirit but a human, so inevitably hunger took over. Sand stuck to my feet as I strode back to our spot, anticipating what my mother had brought for lunch. Money was always tight so we mostly packed; buying a beach hamburger was a rare treat. Sandwiches wrapped in waxed paper, cucumber sticks, and fruit were laid out before us on the least sandy towel. We tucked in eagerly, brushing away the few pesky grains of sand that clung stubbornly to our food. We passed around a thermos of tepid juice or water and then we hit the waves once more.

Since we only went in up to our knees, no "30-minutes after eating" rule applied. Somewhere in between jumping the waves and lunch Paula and I took our pails down to the shoreline and constructed all kinds of "castles." But that eventually became boring so back into the water we went.

As with all good things, the day at the beach came to an end and it was time to pack up and make our way back to the car. What a miserable endeavor. As our damp towels were folded up, sand inevitably blew into my hair only to disappear into my curls. It stuck to my soggy bathing suit. I flat out hated that. As I wiggled my feet into flip-flops, the straps dug the sand into my skin, making each particle feel like a needle piercing me.

But this was not the worst part. We had to slog back to the car, traversing the sweltering parking lot. Surely it was miles long! When at last we reached our car my mother unlocked it and as the doors were opened a blast of heat knocked us over with its force. Beach gear secured in the trunk, we climbed inside. I immediately put my hands under my thighs to protect them from the searing plastic covering the seat.

The ride home was a replay in reverse of the trip out. Go and stop, go and stop. Already the relief of the water and fun in the sand were a seemingly distant memory. Was all this really worth it?

You bet. And I couldn't wait to do it again.

Ice

A few times during the winter we braved the elements and traveled to the beach. Coats were buttoned up to our necks, which were covered with scarves. All that material pushed against my throat like a garrote. But faced with the unforgiving wind I was glad for the warmth. Echoing our summer forays, gulls still swooped and cawed, waves still crashed, and sand still blew.

Occasionally a few other brave souls walked past us, bent against the wind. We raised mittened hands to greet these fellow adventurers, but for the most part the beach was empty. Oddly, I enjoyed these times. The wind was so bracing I felt my face turning red, and then numb. The boardwalk was brittle with cold, and cracked and creaked under our boots.

Eventually we wandered into the café and ordered cups of clam chowder. Just the ticket! As our insides warmed, our outsides defrosted. We watched the ocean through steamy windows. If we lingered long enough, Mommy got coffee and Paula and I were treated to hot chocolate sporting high hats of whipped cream. I imagined that if Marie and her nutcracker prince had been transported to a different Land of Sweets, this was it.

Streams of Adventure

On summer days when we didn't go to the beach Paula and I devised another way to beat the heat. We only had one bike between the two of us, a model with a "banana seat," meaning it was long enough to fit two riders. I was the chauffeur and Paula was the passenger. We pedaled to the end of Liberty Avenue where the woods curved around. A stream wound its way through the leafy coolness. We parked the bike and began to explore.

All manner of interesting detritus floated along the surface: decayed leaves, skinny twisted twigs, strings of emerald green vegetation. The sun filtered through the leaf canopy and dotted the water with sparkling orbs. Here and there the stream sang out as it meandered over a rock. Pebbles smoothed by the continuous washing lined the stream bed. If we were lucky we would spot tadpoles.

Sitting with our feet in the water, we chewed on refreshing spears of cucumber and imagined the life of the mystical creatures that must be hiding from us. We made up stories of the elves and sprites and nymphs that must play and cavort when unencumbered by human presence.

A magical time indeed.

Martians and the Blessed Virgin Mary

At some point, my uncle Bobby came to live with us again. He had been cohabiting with a woman named Shirley who had four kids: Mary, Cindy, Andy, and Ralph. I loved playing with them—they were the closest thing to cousins that I had. We got along so well and we even had sleepovers from time to time. Unsurprisingly, things didn't work out between Bobby and their mother, which is why he now lived with us. He moved into one of the rooms in our attic and, sadly, that was the end of our fairy land.

Our aunt Wendy's dresses were packed away to be replaced by a chess board and Bobby's ham radio contraption. At varying hours of both day and night we heard him yelling, "Breaker, breaker," into the hand-held microphone as he connected with people from all over the world.

It was during this time that I decided I was too old to have a "baby" sister sharing my room. I wanted a bedroom to myself. Amazingly, my mother agreed and set about creating a space for Paula in the attic next to Bobby's. First order of business? Decorate it.

My mother bought a few cans of spray paint in various hues of blue, and no graffiti artist could do any better. Where once there were flat, uninteresting walls of boring off-white now there were swirls and waves of azure and periwinkle and teal. It was as if sky and sea had met in happy circumstance.

The disassembled bunk bed, a dresser, some toys and books, and voila! All was readied for my sister. There was only one drawback: Paula did not want to be up there. After a few nights she pleaded with my mother to let her come back down with us. She cried, she implored, but to no avail. What could possibly be wrong? She had her own space, and it was adorable.

No, she told my mother emphatically. It's not safe up there—Martians snuck into her room at night. This was, no pun intended, completely out of the blue. We were strict Catholics and there was no place in our lives for anything smacking of science fiction. We didn't believe in aliens. We didn't watch *The Outer Limits* or *The Twilight Zone*. We didn't even dress up as witches or ghosts on Halloween. Where did this come from?

I had my own chilling and seemingly inexplicable encounters around this time. One evening, while washing the dishes, a movement attracted my attention. I glanced to my right to look down the short, darkened hallway. The Virgin Mary was coming toward me! I wasn't afraid because—as a good Catholic girl—I believed in and loved the Blessed Mother.

To compound the puzzlement, one evening I woke from a sound sleep and who should be walking toward my bed? None other than Santa Claus! Again, I wasn't afraid because Santa is a good guy who brings us good things.

It wasn't until years later, when I was in therapy, did I learn that children use their imagination to avoid—or even deny—a dangerous or scary experience… or person. They protect themselves by turning the approach of a threatening person into that of a "safe" one. So if, for example, a certain uncle were to approach a vulnerable, defenseless niece, he might be presented, in that niece's mind, as a religious or mythical or otherworldly, but always benign, creature.

The dichotomy here is that said uncle was also a particular favorite of mine. Since there was no father in the home (more about that later) I was thrilled to have Bobby living with us. I actually felt honored, like he *chose* us. And he was great fun. He played Mille Bornes with me if I begged him long enough. (I was sure I was the only one in my school clever enough to play a French card game.)

One morning at breakfast I turned the milk carton, reading each side.

"What does 'equal opportunity farms' mean?" I asked.

Quick as you like, Bobby shot back, "That means they milk black and white cows."

I had a good laugh over that.

Once, my sister, who has a strong artistic bent, asked him to show her how to draw a man. He grabbed her paper and pencil and put a dot in the middle of the sheet.

"There you go," he said. "That's a man two miles away."

Guffaw.

He was a trained artist who had studied at the School of Visual Arts in Manhattan. An encyclopedic mind allowed him to regale us with the most fascinating bits of information.

He was a black belt in judo, a swimming and diving instructor, and an accomplished fisherman. The *Daily News* wrote of his fishing exploits in the sports section. He eventually became a charter boat captain and later earned his private pilot's license. He was also an amazing cook. In a corner of our yard he farmed a vegetable garden that grew abundantly. And I adored him. So much so that when I got married I asked him to walk me down the aisle.

Kissing Cousins

When Bobby first moved in with Shirley it opened a new chapter in my life. I enjoyed visiting my "cousins" because they had cool things that I didn't. "Fizzies" that turned plain water into a bubbly, flavored drink. Music posters on their bedroom walls. A rainbow of nail polishes. (Well, the girls, that is.) Mostly, though, I just remember laughing a lot.

Bobby had dogs penned up in the backyard. Big dogs. The poor things lived on a fenced-in concrete slab with a couple of derelict dog houses for them to cram into. The slab was never cleaned so poop dotted it here and there. The smell was awful and it attracted green, iridescent flies.

While we were playing in the yard a dog began howling. Startled, I looked over to see if it was hurt. *Was* it hurt? Was it *playing*? One dog was mounted on top of the other. It was moving funny. I didn't know what I was seeing but it made me feel queasy. The other kids didn't blink an eye. I guess they were used to it.

That evening we stayed for dinner. We had chicken and mashed potatoes. What made such an unremarkable meal memorable is that Shirley's mother was there as well, a short round woman with puckered lips due to a lack of teeth. She didn't say much—I don't think she spoke English.

Serving us our mashed potatoes, she held a big battered pot from which she scooped out generous spoonfuls. She then took a stick of butter and proceeded to garnish the potatoes, which would have been fine, except she used her hands to squish off a portion of butter and then smash it into our potatoes with her fingers! I was too flabbergasted to even wonder if she had washed her hands. It definitely was… an experience.

After a fun-filled day of playing at my house with Mary and Cindy the time eventually came for them to leave. Apparently I said or did something that set my mother off. She gave me a tongue-lashing, which made me quake. Not because of the volume but because of the rage, the vitriol, the unchecked anger that poured out of her. And she did this right in front of my cousins!

I burst into tears and ran to my room, slid open the door of my closet and sank to my knees. My heart split in two and I felt there were worms rolling around my insides. Pushing myself half into my closet I sobbed. Great, heaving, ugly sobs.

"Why does she always do this to me?" I keened. "Why does she always do this to me?"

I felt a hand on my shoulder and saw Mary standing close behind me. Now on top of every other emotion I was embarrassed to the core. My distress was so… naked. So exposed. Mary tip-toed out after a moment, and I was left to comfort myself. Alone and hiding, halfway in my closet.

Bobby moved in not long after this experience.

"Shirley, that crazy bitch," he growled. "I woke up one night to see her standing over me with a big knife in her hand. She was going to kill me!"

I never saw Mary or Cindy or Andy or Ralph again.

Wedded "Bliss"

My parents had been married in Ft. Dix, New Jersey. My Catholic mother requested that a priest perform the somber ceremony, such as it was, but because my father was Jewish, there was a rabbi waiting in the wings in case the priest objected and therefore refused to perform the marriage. As it turned out, the ceremony proceeded without a hitch. The only people present, except for the celebrants and the priest, were two witnesses.

There was only one picture of my mother in her "wedding" dress. I use quotation marks here because it was not a traditional wedding dress in any sense of the word. It wasn't white. It wasn't floor length. There was no matching veil. Not a sequin or pearl to be found. It was actually fawn-colored with a slim strip of embroidered flowers down the middle of the bodice. She even wore it to her classroom a few times. As for the ring, well, I was curious about that. One day, I must have been about six years old, when I asked in total innocence, "Mommy, where is your wedding ring?"

Without looking at me, as was her habit, she replied, "I sold it to buy you and Paula Christmas presents."

My little heart broke. Not because she had to sell her wedding ring but because my sister and I were the *cause* for the selling of her ring. The guilt of this burden, the knowledge that she had no ring, no reminder of my father, that it was my fault, haunted me for years. What weight to lay upon such young shoulders. Her bitterness and frustration were foisted upon me and I resented it when I became older and thought about this with more mature eyes.

Collecting for Leukemia

My parents divorced when I was little more than three years old so naturally I had no memory of him. My mother manipulated his death to garner sympathy; she martyred herself by claiming to be a widow. It wasn't until I was in my 50s (!) that it dawned on me that she had never been a widow but was, in fact, a divorcée. My father remarried, but died shortly thereafter. Leukemia claimed him when he was not even 30 years old.

My mother told my sister and me that the disease was diagnosed when he'd had a tooth pulled and his gum refused to stop bleeding. (This easily explains why, during my first ever trip to the dentist, I was petrified to the degree that I vomited in the little basin that is reserved for genteel and discreet spitting.)

In any event, this was not the case at all. In my 40s I found the woman he had been married to at the time of his death and she told me how things had actually transpired. He indeed had died of leukemia, but no teeth nor dentist was involved.

All this background is by way of explaining this minor — but indelible — event that occurred when I was in the fourth grade and Paula was in the second. My mother received a fundraising appeal from the Leukemia Society. Eager to contribute, but not to the extent to which she would actively participate, she sent my sister and me out to walk the neighborhood and collect money for The Cause.

She demonstrated how to fill out the envelope with each contributor's name and the amount of their donation, and sent us out with instructions to appeal to people's emotions and, of course, their pocketbooks.

"Tell them your father died of leukemia and your widowed mother is raising you by herself," she instructed.

This engendered several internal reactions in me. On the surface I felt embarrassed—no, that's not the right word... *mortified*—to reveal to strangers such an intimate family detail. I was painfully, cripplingly shy, and to knock on a stranger's door in and of itself was a torturous exercise. I was afraid of failing and not living up to my mother's expectation of an envelope bulging with Loot for Leukemia.

But deeper down, I struggled with the conflict this whole episode wrought. My mother never spoke in warm or nostalgic terms about my father. In fact, my sister and I were not allowed to refer to him as anything other than his first name, as if he were someone alien to us. The first time I timidly (testing the waters) referred to him as "my daddy" my mother got That Look on her face, which made every little hair on the back of my neck stand up.

"That man was no father to you. You are to call him Leon," she replied through clenched teeth.

My little heart hurt, and never again did I employ that treasured, tender term of endearment. I couldn't put my feelings into words, but analyzing it now, I understand that it felt like a betrayal of my father.

He was not good enough to be called my daddy, but I could use him as a means of getting money.

Mea Culpa, Part 2

Father Torquemada and Absolution
Being devout Catholics, all the sacraments, church holidays, and Holy Days of Obligation were observed. We belonged to the local parish, Our Lady of Lourdes. As a second grader, I prepared to make my First Holy Communion. This involved catechism instruction and making my First Confession.

The communion dress, veil, shoes, gloves, rosary beads, and missal were purchased. Shirley was still on the scene at this point, and bought my bouquet—a sweet-smelling collection of roses and baby's breath with a darling fuzzy bee attached.

The Saturday before mass, all us second graders gathered in the pews of Our Lady of Lourdes to receive last instructions before making First Confession, a prerequisite to the Communion ceremony. The local pastor, Father Toomey, was to address us.

Father Toomey was Torquemada reincarnated. His name befit his appearance. He was old and skinny, with black-rimmed glasses that made his eyes bulge out, and cropped white hair spiked atop his head. He seemed all angles; there was nothing soft about him in his black cassock and stiff white collar. He paced back and forth on the altar as he spoke. Spoke? Perhaps I should say he shrieked—even his voice was sharp.

"You children are evil! If you were to die and be thirsting in Purgatory I would not even give you a drop of water! This will be your opportunity to confess all your sins and pray that God will forgive you!"

Whereas holy water is sprinkled during mass, spittle flew from his mouth, defiling the very place that should be the symbol of love, mercy, and grace. And that was merely the introduction; his tirade became more vituperous and vitriolic from there. It's amazing the pews didn't become unhinged from the floor as all us little communicants shook in fear.

Eventually, Father Toomey released us from his rant and we little irredeemable sinners made our way to the confessionals. Desperately trying to come up with a list of wrongs I had committed in my eight years, I settled on what (probably) every other eight year old came up with: I disobeyed my mother; I was mean to my sister; I lied when I said I finished my homework; and so on.

The line was whittling down… there were only three more kids in front of me.

Two kids.

One.

My turn.

I timorously turned the door handle to the confessional. I took one step in, shut the door, and knelt down. I was alone. It was dark.

Suddenly the screen placed between the priest and me slid across and I vaguely saw the shadow of the man who held the power to absolve me of all my sins.

"Bless me, Father, for I have sinned. This is my first confession," I whispered almost inaudibly.

Mysteriously, unexpectedly, suddenly, I felt true contrition for all the ways I had failed God.

Fear was gone, faith filled my soul.

God loved me and forgave all my failings. I believe this was the little mustard seed planted in my eight-year-old heart that took decades to bloom. Where had this come from? I was too young to dissect or analyze this feeling but now I know it was the Holy Spirit, calling me to belong to Jesus.

The priest gave me absolution and assigned the penance I was to perform. Something about this many Hail Marys and that many Our Fathers. There may have been an Act of Contrition thrown in there, too.

I went back to my pew, folded my hands in the correct posture (palms together, fingers pointed skyward toward God, thumbs laid one over the other to mimic the cross) and recited my prayers. Confessed, chastised, and absolved I left the church. Enveloped in the brilliance and purity of the spring day I walked home, lighthearted and in a high state of anticipation. *Tomorrow is Communion Day! Family is coming!* And I would become a true child of God by participating in the most sacred of the sacraments.

Now in those days, Catholics receiving Communion were not permitted to eat anything after midnight, which meant no breakfast. You see, your stomach had to be emptied in order to receive the Body of Christ; the idea was physical hunger would be assuaged by being spiritually fed. But theology means nothing to a hungry little girl.

The Bride of Christ

First Holy Communion

The day having arrived, I dressed with special care and help from my mother. She adjusted my veil so it flowed over my shoulders and the crystal encrusted crown sparkled to perfection. I pulled dainty gloves over my clammy palms. Grasping bouquet, missal, and rosary I got in our car and Mommy, Paula, and I drove off. My grandparents had arrived some time during the preparations and they followed.

All the little brides of Christ floated up the aisles in their white dresses (symbolizing purity) to sit in the section reserved for the communicants. The brides of Christ sat separate from the… what were the little boys called? Nothing special, as far as I know. Our area was awash with flowers and whispers. Incense filled the air. Soft organ music floated down from the loft. The occasional clatter was heard as rosary beads were dropped. Parents and grandparents strained their necks looking for their girl or boy. They pointed or surreptitiously waggled fingers in an attempt to wave at their child, yet still observe the solemnity of the event.

The priest and altar boys made their appearance. Mass was underway.

At the appropriate time, we little lambs were led to the altar, row by row, to receive the Sacrament. As the line inched toward the priest with the wafers, I rehearsed in my mind the protocol. The priest will say, "The body of Christ," at which time I should tilt my head back ever so slightly, and with eyes closed, reply, "Amen." At this point I should then stick out my tongue to receive the Eucharist.

What if I lost my balance with my eyes closed? What if I didn't stick out my tongue far enough and the Eucharist fell on the floor? What if I forgot what I was supposed to say? What if I forgot which pew I was supposed to return to? I was filled with trepidation.

Now it was my turn. I stood in front of the priest, who held the gold paten filled with wafers. Lights bounced off the metallic thread in his vestments. Wisps of incense swirled behind him. Altar boys stood solemnly at each side. The scene was ethereal.

"Body of Christ," he said reverently, and almost imperceptibly I responded, "Amen."

I did it. Filled with grateful relief I made it back to my pew and lowered myself to the kneeler. Careful not to bite or chew the wafer, I allowed it to slowly and reverently dissolve in my mouth.

After all the children had received Communion it was now time for the adults who wished to participate. The priest returned to the altar, wiped out the cup and performed all the other rituals that follow Communion. After the last few words in Latin were spoken, the triumphant strains of the recessional were played and we trooped out of the church. Mass was over.

An Unholy Ending

Families reunited and all made their way to cars to drive off to a celebratory meal. Since this was a special day, a special meal was in order, and restaurants were especially busy. As for us, we went to one of the local diners. My mother, sister, grandmother, grandfather, and I crammed into a booth. Even though it was now early afternoon, we opted for breakfast rather than lunch. Steaming cups of coffee were brought to the adults, and even though I didn't like milk, that was ordered for my sister and me.

It seemed like a week had passed since I had eaten. My stomach growled incessantly and I felt slightly dizzy. We gave our orders to the waitress and waited for the food to come. Things between my mother and her parents were always—to put it nicely—tense, and although they made an effort for my sake, the undercurrent of a possible explosion was palpable, adding to my discomfort.

At last our food came. I had asked for over easy eggs, but to my deep disappointment they were as undercooked as Miss Evelyn's. The yolks were too jiggly and there were strands of uncooked whites that looked like snot shimmering over the surface. I gamely ate a few forkfuls but even though the bread was toasted and buttered to perfection, it was not enough to calm my stomach.

Queasiness forced its way up my throat. I hurriedly asked to go to the bathroom and without waiting for permission, veil whipping behind me, I walked as fast as possible. Slamming the stall door behind me, and barely getting it latched shut, I turned around and threw up.

Heaving and retching, I then started crying. I was doomed! Damned! I had thrown up Jesus!

It was one of the blackest moments of my eight years. When I returned to the table, thankfully, nobody noticed that my eyes were red and I was softly hiccupping. It was my only moment of true relief that morning.

After everyone else had finished eating, we made our way to the parking lot. My mother said a curt farewell to her parents while I gave my grandparents a hug. My grandfather slipped me the customary dollar "for ice cream" and he and my grandmother got in their car and drove off to the Bronx. We went home as well, where I divested myself of the bridal assemblage. I was exhausted.

Tempting the Priest

Having made my First Communion, I was now allowed to participate in the sacrament every Sunday. Saturday afternoons my mother and I went to church to make our confessions. It was so hard, week after week, to come up with new sins. Regardless, every seven days a new Sunday morning dawned and back to church we went to Mass.

One particular Sunday my mother sat us up at the front of the church. Being that this was the 1960s, females did not wear pants to church; it was strictly dresses only. So there we were, in the first pew, in our dresses. I was rutching around, trying to keep the itchy voile of the slip from irritating my legs.

My mother leaned over to me. The perpetual frown between her eyes looked like a knife had split her forehead as it deepened. "Put your legs together," she admonished in a pseudo-whisper. "Sitting like that could tempt the priest. He might look up your dress!"

I slapped my knees together—*I will not be the cause of the priest's sinning!* I have often thought about this and even today am perplexed by it. Did my mother truly think a priest would be excited by a little girl's panties? Or was there some dark and depraved attitude toward men and sex that had been shaped early in her girlhood?

The answer is as mysterious as transubstantiation.

Music Lessons

Not the Lady of Spain

Music has always played a central role in my life. It is so much more than background noise, or a scene-setter for a party, or a solution to bring on sleep. If music is playing, my conscious mind is fully engaged. I cannot listen to music if I'm studying or performing a demanding task because my mind will be pulled, magnetically connecting the sound waves and my brain.

I come by this honestly; my mother always played music on either the radio or the turntable, and my father was an amateur opera singer. I can remember singing along to arias when I was yet in elementary school.

One of my earliest memories is of music. My mother owned a recording, a 33 1/3 LP of Mozart's opera *The Magic Flute*. On side two, the very first aria was sung by the Queen of the Night. I couldn't get enough of it. The soaring notes, the emotion, the tension gripped me and held me captive. I lay on the floor with the turntable plugged into the wall and played that aria over and over. As soon as it finished I lifted the arm of the record player and started it anew.

First came the scratchiness common to all records. Then the initial chord of the orchestra sounded... not timidly but storming into the aria, warning the listener that what was to come was emotionally wrought and from the gut of the character. I must have been about four because this was when we lived in Queens.

In the inevitable progression of events, when I was eight my mother decided I should have music lessons. And what instrument did she pick for me? Not the delicate flute. Not the sweet violin. Not the obligatory piano.

No, she decided I should play the accordion.

The squeeze box.

She purchased a beautiful ruby red instrument ornamented with a pearlescent swirl. To hold the music books she bought a wobbly metal music stand. Mr. Massano, the music teacher from Manetuck Elementary, had a second-floor studio in Babylon and was hired.

Because the accordion itself emptied the coffers, there was no money left over to purchase a case. So each week I lugged the accordion, shrouded in a pillowcase, up the stairs for my lesson. I strapped the instrument on and played for the teacher. He taught me scales, timing, and how to read music. Two songs I played (*not* "Lady of Spain!") are "Everybody Loves Somebody Sometime" — a big hit for Dean Martin — and "Santa Lucia."

I had an affinity for playing, as long as I didn't have an audience. To practice, I went in my room and shut the door. If I heard even the mailman coming I stopped playing.

"Keep going!" my mother yelled from the kitchen. "The mailman doesn't care about your practicing!"

So being obedient, I played, but trembling and timorous.

Eager to show off my talents, my mother insisted I play while her friend, Alyce (more about her later), came over. "Wait till you hear Ellen play!" my mother gushed. (There was an unspoken competition between my mother and Alyce over their elder daughters.) Reluctantly I dragged out the accordion and looped the cushioned straps over each shoulder. I set the rickety stand on its tripod legs and shakily put a piece of sheet music on it.

Nerve endings in my hands tingled and my palms and fingers began to sweat. The notes blurred as I started to cry.

"Go in the corner and turn around. Pretend no one is here, that you're just by yourself," was my mother's solution.

Standing in the corner, tears coursing down my reddened cheeks, nose swelling up, I rendered an anemic version of some song.

Not too long after, the pillowcase was replaced with a bona fide black carrying case that was lined in blood red velvet. It was pretty snazzy, but not enough to make up for the embarrassment I felt dragging it around.

Oddly enough, today I enjoy the accordion — hearing it in ethnic, folk, or even classical music — but not playing it. The experience so affected me that even today, taking piano lessons as an adult, my hands get clammy and I long for a corner to stand in.

There's Gas in the Basement

My mother seemed to like Mr. Massano. A lot. He was a soft-spoken gentle man with a pleasant personality. My mother told me he was a widower (she had to explain what that meant) with one daughter. I believe my mother thought a romance might develop. She invited him to dinner and he accepted. I was happy because somehow I intuited my mother's intentions, and that was fine by me. I so badly wanted a father.

A particular incident during that meal involved a bowl of pitted black olives. Paula snuck ten of them and stealthily inserted one olive over each of her fingertips. Drawing her hands from under the table, where her ploy had been executed, she held them up and waggled her fingers at Mr. Massano. I laughed. Mr. Massano smiled benignly. My mother frowned.

Soon after, my music lessons with Mr. Massano abruptly came to an end. Was he so aghast by our bad table manners? Had Paula and I ruined everything? Or was it a money issue? I was never told the reason. My mother subsequently found another teacher whose name I don't remember.

Whereas Mr. Massano's studio was in town, and bright with the light of day, this teacher's studio was in his home, in his basement. It was dark and it smelled. Really bad, like mildew, and old carpeting, and... At the time I didn't know what it was called, but now I know he had a colostomy bag.

He also had gas. Lots of it.

So I sat on an old metal chair with a kitchen towel safety-pinned to the plastic-covered seat, played through my lesson, and tried to inhale as shallowly as possible. Occasionally he had other kids over with whatever instrument they were learning and we engaged in a jam session.

There was a certain boy in the group, and I thought he was the coolest thing. He played the guitar. His hair fell across his forehead just like one of the Beatles. He sat hunched over, and had a habit of pushing his cheek out with his tongue. I thought he was right up there with Paul McCartney (my favorite Beatle). I tried emulating him, but somehow it wasn't as cool with an accordion fastened to my chest. After our lesson we waited outside (ah—fresh air!) for our parents and I tried my best to get his attention but, alas, never succeeded.

In due course my lessons inexplicably came to an end. The accordion somehow vanished and I never learned its fate.

It's a Beautiful Morning

My love of music wasn't restricted to the classical genre. Although that is what was mostly heard in our house, at times my mother played folk music: The Weavers; The Highwaymen; Peter, Paul, and Mary; Burl Ives; Woody Guthrie—I loved them all. I wonder if my mother ever became cognizant that they were mostly of the Communist bent.

I had my own burgeoning tastes, too. One of my favorites was "It's a Beautiful Morning" by The Rascals. I just loved it, especially the intro of tinkling wind chimes.

I had a little hand-held transistor radio that tuned in AM stations. When the song came on, if my mother wasn't around I turned up the volume. Eyes closed, I swayed to the music as images of sunshine, fields of flowers, and birds filled my mind. I felt like I could float over a meadow as lightly as a butterfly.

For weeks I saved up my allowance and finally had sufficient funds to buy my very own copy. Not enough for the whole album, only the 45. My very first record, all my own!

I played this on the record player and danced in my room. But secretly, because "rock 'n roll" wasn't allowed in our house. One day when my mother was out, I had the volume turned up and was immersed in the music. I was so engaged that I didn't hear her return. She stormed down the hall and opened my door with a bang.

"Give me that garbage!" she demanded, open hand extended imperiously.

I relinquished my precious record, which immediately went into the trash. My chest swelled with anger, despair, impotence.

"I bought that record! It's mine! You have no right to take it! You don't have to listen to it if you don't want to!"

But she heard none of what I said, it was all just exploding in my mind—one simply did not talk back to my mother.

We're Famous!
Even though my mother never listened to AM radio she somehow discovered that the local station (which ironically often played "It's a Beautiful Morning") was soliciting funds for some local emergency. She decided we would contribute, not only as a gesture of good citizenship, but also as a lesson for Paula and me about tangibly

caring for others. We brought our piggy banks to the station and emptied them on the receptionist's desk. On the way home my mother tuned the radio to the station and we heard our names announced. Paula and I were thrilled! We were local celebrities. More importantly, we learned that displaying kindness and concern for others in a demonstrable way actually felt good. Mommy taught us a valuable lesson that morning.

We also learned that it was easier for Mommy to love people on the other side of the world than those in her own life.

That Which Doesn't Kill You…

A Red Wagon and Ammonia
When we moved from West Islip to North Babylon we no longer had a washer or dryer in the house. Luckily, in the little town, which was only the length of two sidewalks, there was a laundromat. My mother occasionally sent me to do the laundry. She separated it into whites, darks, and colors, and wrote down the directions for each load. The piles were shoved into pillowcases—no longer needed as an accordion case, now repurposed into laundry sacks. Notes pinned on each, Mommy lined them up in the bed of a creaky red wagon and squeezed in a box of laundry detergent. Off I went.

On the occasions when we ran out of soap, my mother gave me a handful of dimes and nickels for the detergent machines. I loved easing the coins into the appropriate slots and determining which box of powder to select.

"Tide." That was a good one—I imagined waves of cleanliness swooshing over our clothes.

"All." All the dirt will be gone.

"Sail." The dirt will simply sail away! And I got to choose!

One day my mother prepared everything. I got the requisite list, with one new item on it: ammonia. "This bottle is for the muddy gardening clothes," she instructed. Then she issued a warning.

"Whatever you do, don't sniff it because it's really strong."

Hauling the trusty wagon behind me I squeaked my way to the laundromat. I dumped the contents of each pillowcase in machines, added the soap, and grabbed the bottle of ammonia. I uncapped it.

It can't be that *bad*, I thought. Innocence and curiosity mingled like soap and water.

I lifted the gray plastic bottle to my nose and sniffed. Not a cursory sniff but as deep a lungful as an asthmatic might inhale steroids.

I immediately lost my vision.

My sinuses burst into flames.

Without knowing what I was doing I dropped the bottle and ran blindly for the door. Outside, I bent over, grabbed my knees for support, and gulped air. Oh, but it hurt! A concerned woman followed me and asked if I was all right.

I barely registered what she was saying but I managed to nod yes. Eventually.

When the driers stopped spinning—and my head cleared, my eyes stopped stinging and tearing, and my breathing returned to normal—I shoved the clothes back into the pillowcases. I lined them up in the wagon and, wheels squealing behind me, pulled the whole shebang home.

Mommy never noticed my red eyes and runny nose.

The Manhattan Experience

50 Carmine

50 Carmine Street was a special place—a six-story Romanesque-revival residential building completed in 1896, owned by my great-grandmother Irene. My great-aunt Louise lived there with her, in the first-floor apartment. My mother, father, and I also lived there after my father's stint at Ft. Benning in Georgia was up.

50 Carmine Street exterior (left).
The kitchen with Gramma Irene, Alfred, Lucy, and Louis (right).

When my sister was born in St. Vincent's Hospital she rounded out our family. One unique feature of the apartment was the dual-purpose kitchen table. When the tabletop was lifted up, there was a bathtub underneath!

Blowing bubbles on the fire escape.

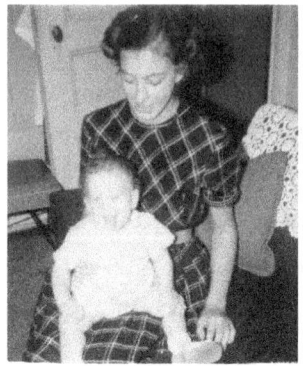 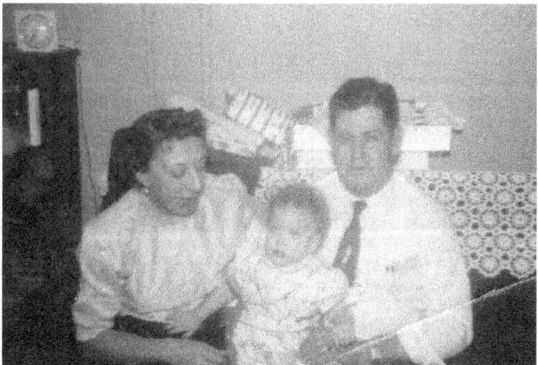

Newly returned from Georgia.
Mommy and me (left), and Mom and Morris with me (right).

The only picture of me and my paternal grandmother, Santina (left).
My father (center).
Feeding the pigeons in Washington Square Park (right).

Bathing in the kitchen table (left).
On the carousel in Central Park, wearing the coat my grandmother sewed.

After we made the move to Long Island, we regularly came into the City to visit Gramma Irene and Louise. Sometimes we took the Long Island Rail Road (LIRR). Most often, though, my mother drove. With expert technique Mommy slid the car (she was still driving The Tank) into the first spot she found on a street—all without power steering! Parking lots cost money so that option was out of the question. Besides, finding a free spot was a badge of honor to any self-respecting New Yorker.

We walked a block or two until we got to Carmine Street, passing produce carts, bakeries, record shops, restaurants, dry goods stores, pharmacies, and fortune tellers. At number 50 we opened the door and entered the tiny foyer. The floor was covered with black and white octagonal tiles. It wasn't very big, merely enough to have mailboxes recessed into two walls and a buzzer for each apartment. Paula and I stood patiently while Mommy buzzed "Zanelli" and waited for the locked hallway door to click open. We then got our first whiff.

Unless you have entered into an old, West Village apartment building, it's difficult, if not impossible, to describe the smell—a combination of old bricks and mortar, cooking, mustiness, and the ephemera of past residents.

In this case, there were two particular odors. In addition to owning the building, Gramma Irene also owned the adjoining storefront. This was occupied by an Italian tradesman who made pungent salamis and dried sausages. The other smell came from the second apartment on the first floor which was rented to a woman named Madeleine. She was old, and eccentric in the uniquely Lower Manhattan way, and took in any stray cat she came across on her forays. There are a lot of stray cats in Manhattan.

So as you may imagine, this building had a very particular… aroma, all its own. As a young child, however, I didn't pass any judgment—this was just the way it was. In any event, I was too excited to see

Gramma Irene and my great-aunt Louise to ascribe any value, good or bad.

Abacus and Espresso

Black and white tiles continued from the foyer onto the hallway floors. The wall was painted a dull olive green and had a bumpy texture. I ran my fingers along it as we made our way to the stairs. There were four steps to reach the first small landing. Each marble stair was well worn in the middle, witness to generations who had trod up and down. A curved wooden handrail, supported by wrought iron posts, was shiny from the many hands that had slid along it over the decades. About eight more steps from the landing and we were on the first floor. One right turn into a dark alcove and we were arrived.

The door opened, and there stood Gramma Irene, beaming at us, her two little jewels. She was short—not much taller than I was at age six—and round, the snaps of her housecoat straining across her ample bosom. She had shiny silver hair, but since it was always wound into a bun, I never knew its length. She had the most beautiful complexion, lightly olive, with barely a wrinkle, even though she was 80-something years old. She gave each of us a hug, and what a hug! Her love squeezed the breath out of you! As she embraced us she murmured words of joy in Italian into our ears. Louise, much less expressive, simply smiled and asked about our trip into the City.

The apartment was old, and probably had never changed since the Zanellis first occupied it, or maybe even before then. One entered the kitchen. The ceilings were high, probably 10 feet. The cabinets over the sink extended all the way up, and were fronted with glass panes. The sink was porcelain, shallow, and yellowed with age. There was a ridiculously narrow stove in front of the grimy window, which was never opened and looked out onto a sliver of an alley. Incongruently, a dusty abacus was propped on the ledge.

Always, always, there was the battered, dull metal espresso pot standing sentry on one of the burners. A wooden table was to the left of the stove, and behind it, to the right of the door, was an old chest with a radio and some trifles. (My mother said when she lived there she would tune in to *The Lone Ranger* — in Italian. The Ranger's horse was named Morelli, and instead of saying "Hi ho Silver, away!" this Ranger yelled, "Avanti, Morelli!")

Gramma Irene made espresso, and poured me half a cup, stirred in some raw sugar and topped it off with milk. Then wielding the big serrated knife, she cut a slice of bread from a loaf that was the size of a car tire. She slathered it with butter — always unsalted, whipped butter from a blue waxed cardboard tub, never a stick — and told me to dunk it in the coffee.

Ah, heaven. Caffeinated, cholesterolled heaven. One had to have strong teeth to eat that bread. It was the real deal — a crust that fought back, and a dense and chewy inside. The bread came from Zito's on Bleecker Street.

Baldwin and Remington

The tiny rectangular room off the kitchen had a desk and an upright piano. That's about all that fit! This was the next best place to be, after the kitchen. My mother, Gramma Irene, and Louise sat in the adjoining living room and chatted. By turns, I plunked on the Baldwin piano (it was very tall!) and played "secretary" at the desk.

A black Remington typewriter sat on it elegantly. There were sheets of pristine white paper stacked in one of the drawers. I took one sheet, inserted it into the space between the roller and back of the machine, and started scrolling to feed the paper. Careful! Oh, it went in a little crooked… unwind and start over. Ah, that's better. Satisfied, I wrote a note, fascinated by the shadowed, blurry-edged letters that appeared, courtesy of each rounded key. They were not unlike the keys of the register at the dry cleaners.

What did I write? Who knows? But whatever the content, it was vitally important to me. It came from my imagination, from my heart, and every grownup in the living room got their own missive. Each individual letter was unspooled from the typewriter, at which point I folded it carefully in thirds, running my fingernail down each crease to make it sharp. Hand delivered, the recipient oohed and aahed over her very own note. It was great fun and had I known who Ernest Hemingway was, I would have felt his equal.

Into the Catacomb

Beyond the living room were the bedroom and then an additional room. This gloomy area was sparsely furnished with a tub and a long, dusty dresser. The tub was a deep, white cast iron affair overlaid with porcelain and balanced atop claw feet. It had a rubber stopper held by a ball chain to fit in the drain. A little metal soap rack was hooked over one side of the tub which held leftover slivers of soap. They were to be rubbed over a washcloth so every little splinter was used up.

The dresser is what held my fascination, though. Louise had the most beautiful, impressive collection of tiny glass perfume bottles. Some boasted painted butterflies, others had dainty porcelain flowers attached. Some were clear and some were vivid with translucent colors. The perpetual semi-dark of the room was due to the absence of windows, but the presence of a bare light bulb, operated by yanking on a frayed string, caused that assemblage to capture what little light was available and sparkle like a queen's jewels.

Louise was petite and had the body of a ballerina, which was appropriate since she had been a dancer in her youth; she'd actually held a recital at Carnegie Hall. She had fine chestnut brown hair that she wore in a plain style.

Gramma Irene died when I was in the second grade; I watched my mother get dressed to go to her funeral and wished I could go with her. My seven-year-old heart thumped with sadness. Gramma was in my life for a short while, but I loved her and felt her passing deeply.

Louise en pointe in character.

A Kidney and a Radio

Whenever we visited Louise we ate out. She never once cooked for us but sometimes had a pot going for her lone meal and it always smelled delicious. One particular aroma made my mouth water, and when I asked her what she was cooking — it smelled divine — she said it was kidney! That gave me the shivers. Anyway, we usually walked to a local restaurant, of which there were so many to choose. True to her former training she led briskly, toes pointed out, while we hurried along to keep up.

Nobody walks faster than a Manhattanite but she really put us through our paces. Before we left her apartment she turned on her radio and propped a note on the table that read: "Dr. Singh, I'll be back in 10 minutes." It was the same piece of paper; she saved it each time for the next outing. She was so afraid someone might break into her apartment. Paranoid, actually. Why? I have no idea. The dust and gloom in her apartment reflected a life that was lived under a shroud of fear and shadowy danger.

Once the radio loudly stood guard on her kitchen table she deemed it safe to leave. Turning keys in two locks on the door she headed down the marble stairs, so sure of her steps that she eschewed the shiny, worn banister.

The gustatory possibilities awaiting us were endless.

The local Italian joints or a Greek place? Should we try that new Indonesian restaurant that opened last week? Do you think we should travel uptown and see what looks interesting?

If we needed to take a cab, Louise kept a close eye on the route the cabbie was taking, ensuring that he did not mistake us for tourists and drive all over the city in order to pad his fare. She sure knew all the tricks.

Whiskey and Diamonds

So, Dr. Singh. When Louise was studying ballet she wanted to learn better breath control and breathing techniques. I don't know how, but she found Dr. Singh, whom I assumed practiced some form of Eastern breathing and exercise. Maybe he had been a yogi? The framed black and white photograph from his youth displayed on her bedroom table featured him in bejeweled Indian garb, playing a long-necked sitar.

Most of the time when we showed up for a visit, Louise called Dr. Singh and had him join us. He had a thick Indian accent and the gray, frizzled hairs in his nose whistled when he exhaled. A short man, he dressed impeccably in a bespoke suit, starched shirt, and silk tie. His tasseled loafers were always polished to a military sheen. And as soon as he got in the door, Louise handed him his customary glass of whiskey, barely diluted with a whisper of water.

He had an inexhaustible supply of stories with which to regale us — sometimes more than once — and as the whiskey in his (second or third) glass went down, the stories became more and more elaborate and fantastical. He laughed at his own recitations; I think he amused himself more than he did any of us. The only story I vaguely remember is something about his time in Hollywood where he found himself at many a party, one of which included a guest, Fatty Arbuckle. What a name! Such a name one does not forget.

Anyway, Louise eventually decided it was time to go and she'd fuss at him:

"Alright, Dr. Singh. Let's go."

He'd keep talking.

She'd take the glass out of his hand and set it on the table with a commanding clink. While he was still talking, head swiveled backward to his audience, she ushered him out the door.

She had known him for many years but I never heard her address him as anything other than Dr. Singh. I actually never knew his first name. And he loved Paula and me. He fawned over us at each visit and promised that when we got older he would write to his family in India and have them send us both a diamond from the family mine.

That letter must have gotten lost in the mail.

During one visit the five of us piled into a taxi and went to the United Nations. Dr. Singh had been employed to translate a film from whatever Indian language had been spoken into English. Apparently there was some editing that had to be done and his voice was needed.

Afterwards, as was our habit, we went to a restaurant, but this time to one on the east side, since that was where we were.

It was so different from the Village. It didn't have the cozy neighborhood feel but was busier and more, I don't know, impersonal? There weren't any narrow, dusty bookstores or herb shops. I didn't see any signs for phrenologists or palm readers. Everything was in English. The people looked different, too. Sikhs in colorful coiled turbans strode the sidewalks. Diplomats from all over the world were evident. I was particularly intrigued by the men wearing tasseled red fezzes, but so glad when we got back to 50 Carmine.

Be that as it may, Dr. Singh was our perpetual guest. Years later, when my daughter was still an infant, he accompanied Louise on her visit by train to Westchester County where I was living. He brought with him the gift of a book he had written on Indian music. The cover was beautiful with a peacock tail spread across a soft silver background, which promised the reader an exotic experience. The contents? Another matter altogether. The antithesis of exotic. They were completely incomprehensible to me. I was able to read music and to count time, but this made no sense whatsoever. During one of our moves, while I was culling our belongings, I got rid of it.

Oddly enough, as much a part of our lives that Dr. Singh was, I don't remember anything about his death. I think Louise called my mother at some point to tell her that he had died, but we weren't involved in his funeral nor did we attend any kind of memorial service. It was very strange. He was there, and then he wasn't. I'm sure Louise was heartbroken though, because as far as I know he was her only friend. She was a solitary person, either by choice or by circumstance. This must have been a very difficult adjustment.

Water Closet Willies

Another oddity about 50 Carmine was that it was missing... a toilet! Inside the apartment, anyway. To use the restroom, one had to secure the skeleton key that hung by the front door, and go out into the hallway. Facing the top of the landing were two doors, side by side. The door on the left belonged to Madeleine's apartment, and the one on the right belonged to us. The key unlocked the door and about three steps in was the toilet. I hated going in there! I had to find the string dangling... somewhere... in front of me... to pull and turn on the light. When my business was finished I had to yank another long chain, this one with a wooden dowel at the end, because the water tank was a wooden box attached high up on the wall over the toilet.

This was as close to an actual water closet—popular in the 1500s in England with the advent of indoor toileting—as one could get. I doubt Carmine Street's facility was much improved upon that medieval phenomenon. I got out of there as quickly as possible, shakily locked the door, and raced back to the apartment, inwardly sighing with relief as I returned the key to its rightful place.

Carmine Street, as we called the apartment, was old and dingy and dirty. The floors were ancient linoleum that at one time had been either green or gray, impossible to tell given their age. They were extremely dusty—not a fine dust to be whisked away with a cloth, but an oily soot that clung tenaciously to the floor, ready to defy any mop that might be applied. The furniture was old, and the occasional roach made its appearance. (OK, more than occasional.) Regardless, I loved that place and the people in it. My memories are stubbornly fond and I am grateful for them.

Old World Meets New World

27 Downing Street as it looks today (left). Bill of sale (right).

The Village, in those days, was exclusively Italian and had been for decades. My great-grandfather, Antonio Zanelli, owned an olive oil and wine import business, located at 27 Downing Street, until Prohibition and the Depression forced him to close shop. Later the beatniks and Communists and gays would make their appearances. Much later, the yuppies and Hollywood types discovered its unique joys. But sadly, maddeningly, their impressive and unmatchable bank accounts drove out all the "old" residents and rendered most of the real estate unattainable for the rest of us.

For the few short years of my childhood though, I reveled in the sounds of Italian being spoken, the aromatic specialty shops with cheeses and sausages and pastas (deVincenzi's had the best homemade ravioli). Fresh, crisp produce, the shoemaker with his intricate machinery and pungent waxes, fragrant flower stalls boasting vibrant blooms year-round, the incredible bakeries featuring treasured recipes from "the Old World," the drinking fountains right on the sidewalks, the cobblestone streets.

Pigeons with iridescent ringed necks strutted along as if they owned the town. Old ladies sat in Father Demo Square and watched the traffic go by, jabbering away in their native tongue. Old men played chess or rustled their *giornali* as they caught up on current events from back home. The bells from Our Lady of Pompeii (where I was baptized) offered dulcet chimes every quarter hour. It was a magical world in which I felt safe and contented. I miss it almost every day.

Our Lady of Pompeii where I was baptized.
It stands on the corner of Carmine and Bleecker Streets.

The Lower East Side

Even though we now lived on Long Island we spent a good deal of time in Manhattan. Sometimes we drove; other times we took the Long Island Railroad, which I especially loved for two reasons — one was that the railroad cars had top and bottom seats, like bunkbeds on wheels. I preferred the top since there was a better view out the window. The other reason was that the train deposited us at Grand Central, a marvelous place. It was a hive of all kinds of activity — commuters, shoppers, buskers, vendors, bakeries, flower shops, a famous oyster bar. We'd make our way out of the platform area, meander through the station, and just a few blocks later we were rewarded with a view of the awe-inspiring marble lions guarding the Manhattan branch of the NYC Library.

Patience and Fortitude are the two lions installed in 1911 in front of the New York City Library.

To get downtown we had the choice of taxi or subway, which in my mind was the better option. Down to a different platform, quick jump in the car before the doors shut, and through the tunnel we went. The lights blinked on and off at certain points (to this day I don't know why) and it felt like we were hurtling toward our destination at 110 miles per hour. To intensify the experience, we could be neck and neck with the train running on the track right next to us. We saw the faces of people in the other cars. It seemed like there was only an inch separating the trains — yikes! — until eventually one or the other veered off in a different direction.

Going to the Lower East Side, though, always meant taking the car. It was easier and more direct. Now, this neighborhood was really something. First of all, we passed by Alphabet City, which was unique in that it is the only part of the City that has single letters for names of the streets — Avenues A, B, C, and D. I will never forget the time driving through the neighborhood during a downpour when a teenage boy stuck his head out of his apartment window, actually shampooing his hair in the rain.

We drove up and down the streets until my mother found on-street parking, passing storefronts and pushcarts heaped with merchandise. If you couldn't find what you were looking for here, it most likely didn't exist. Clothing, pots and pans, shoes, radios, strollers, plastic flowers, beauty products, health aids, umbrellas, cameras... And the food! Nowhere on earth was there better pastrami on rye and half-done pickles.

We walked up and down the streets, following my mother as she examined the different stores and open-air displays. Ah! Here's a cart selling knishes; of course we had to have one, with a choice of yellow or spicy brown mustard — spicy brown for me, thank you.

The mining for treasures completed, we "followed our noses" to a deli and dragged our exhausted bodies and bulging shopping bags inside and collapsed into a booth.

No matter which deli we chose, there was always the metal bowl on the table filled with sour pickles and green tomatoes to chomp on while deciding what to order. For me, there was never a question — it had to be pastrami on rye (seeded) with mustard and a side of coleslaw. And to drink? A fountain chocolate soda, of course.

The waiter, invariably a grumpy older guy with baggy pants and a dirty apron, schlepped over with our food and plopped the dishes on the table. It was like *we* were doing *him* a favor by eating there. But there was no malice behind his gruffness — unless you had the chutzpah to complain. Then you were in for it!

"So, Miss Fancy Pants. Not enough chocolate? Hey Murray (yelling across the entire room to the guy behind the counter), make another soda for the Queen of Sheba here, and don't skimp on the syrup!"

You didn't mind because it was all an act and just the way it was… and the way it should be. All part of the Lower East Side experience.

The one distinctive feature about being in this neighborhood, an element that existed nowhere else in any of the five boroughs, was the abundant evidence of the sad history of many of its residents and workers. Bare arms exposed tattooed numbers, denoting a survivor of a concentration camp. Even at our young ages, the significance and poignancy were not lost on Paula and me. It was sobering since we were very much aware of our father's Jewishness. We easily imagined that relatives of our grandfather—who had come to America from Priluke, Russia—had violently perished during the war.

Ballet and Bali

There were other cultural experiences available to us. My mother was adamant that we appreciate all the City had to offer, including the ballet (Maria Tallchief and Natalia Makarova!) and the opera. We applauded the swirling colors, black-haired beauties, and pounding rhythms of Ballet Folklórico de México. We were mesmerized by the gongs, intonations of monks, and unusual head and hand movements of Indonesian Bali dancers. Many times we walked the galleries of the Metropolitan Museum of Art.

Shrunken heads and the whale hanging from the ceiling of the Museum of Natural History never ceased to amaze. The universe expanded before us in the Hayden Planetarium. We had meals in Greek, Italian, Indian, Chinese, and Pakistani restaurants. We saw Sikhs with colorful turbans walking the same streets as sari-clad women. NYC was a pastiche of sights, sounds, colors, and flavors.

Carp and Pagodas

One of my favorite places was Chinatown. A short taxi ride deposited us into another world. Honey-glazed ducks glistened in restaurant windows. Enormous carp swam in murky tanks, unaware of their fate, waiting to be cooked and served. Alien, extraordinary vegetables were stacked in wooden crates outside grocery shops. Of course, all the writing was in Chinese, and even the telephone booths were shaped like miniature pagodas. The streets were a life-sized kaleidoscope of colors.

We picked a restaurant—it didn't matter which one because every dining room served the most delicious food. After egg rolls, soup, noodles, thinly sliced meats, rice, exotic sauces, and cups of tea, we proceeded to the shops. Jade, umbrellas, cooking utensils, bamboo plants, colorful ceramic urns, silk kimonos—each shop was crammed to the rafters.

In one such store was a display counter of jewelry. I spied a "gold" ring (adjustable band) with a painted red square on top that featured a Chinese character. As we walked down the street I held my hand up to admire the bauble. The letter intrigued me. Did it hold some ancient Chinese wisdom? Did it signify love? Was it a tribal symbol? I decided to ask my mother. She took my hand and studied the character.

"Hmm," she pondered, turning my hand this way and that. "Ah! I think it says, 'Shit on all white people.'"

So much for the mysteries of the East.

The Bronx

Bronx Bombshell

My mother was an attractive woman who did everything possible to make herself unattractive. She never wore makeup, nor jewelry, and during one period of severe despondency wore men's eyeglasses because she "wasn't pretty enough for ladies' frames." She had thick auburn hair that glistened reddish-gold in the sunlight but she often wore it in spartan styles, once even dyeing it a flat, dull black.

Her sister Wendy was eight years her junior and the last in a family of four kids. By the time this child was on the way my poor grandmother had already been supporting her three older children through the post-Depression era and suffering a horrendously abusive marriage. She gave my mother the privilege of naming this new baby and she came up with Wendy. Not short for Gwendolyn, just Wendy.

Left to right, Wendy, Bobby, Ronny, and my mother above.

Wendy was everything my mother wasn't. She was blonde and didn't wear glasses. Her nails—fingers and toes—were beautifully filed and polished. Her clothes were always *au courant* and her shoes were sexy stilettos. Where my mother was stern, Wendy was carefree. As opposed to the hulking steel behemoth my mother drove, Wendy sat behind the wheel of a sleek convertible, a stylish silky kerchief tied loosely under her chin to protect her hair. And I was lucky enough to be her goddaughter.

When I was elementary school age, my grandparents moved from a Manhattan apartment in Washington Heights (that apartment was always referred to as "511") to a semi-detached in the Bronx, on Harding Avenue, where Wendy and my uncle Ronny also lived. During the summers I often stayed over, basking in the warmth of my grandmother's adoration and following my aunt around like a devoted puppy. At the time she worked as an executive secretary in Manhattan at Metropolitan Life in the Flatiron District on East 23rd Street and Lexington Avenue.

If I was up early enough, I watched her get ready for work. Her matching lingerie was a confection of silk and lace. Pencil skirts or A-line dresses looked equally stylish—and sexy—on her. What fascinated me most, though, was how she knotted and pinned her hair into a French twist. No Hollywood actress could compare to her glamour and sophistication. She was my idol and I wanted nothing more than to emulate her.

Back in those days, everyone smoked (except my mother—who admirably never touched a cigarette). One evening, after dinner, I decided to "practice" being Wendy. Everyone was downstairs. My grandmother and my step-grandfather Morris, engaged in their nightly ritual, reading the evening newspaper. Wendy washed the dishes, and Ronny stretched out on the living room floor to watch TV.

Unnoticed, I snuck somebody's cigarette and tiptoed upstairs. I took a scarf from Wendy's dresser, went into the bathroom and locked the door. I tied the scarf lightly around my head like Wendy did. I emptied the plastic cup of its toothbrushes and filled it with water. I then took two Alka-Seltzer tablets from their tin foil packet and dropped them into the water, at which point they burst into fizzy bubbles. With (unlit) cigarette in one hand and my "champagne" in the other, I mimed an animated conversation to myself in the mirror and played "cocktail party."

I felt very grownup and classy and was sure that a real life of social whirlwinds was in my future.

She Got Her Wings

Commuting to Manhattan might have been exciting enough for some people, but Wendy wanted more. Having grown up in the City, it didn't hold the allure it might for others, and sitting behind a desk was stifling and boring to a woman of her adventurous appetite. She applied to Pan American Airlines and was accepted into the stewardess training program. Pan Am was the gold standard in the airline industry. One had to be fluent in a language other than English even to be considered.

Wendy posing in front of a Pan Am turbine.

Wendy had studied Italian in school and also conversed in it with Mom so she spoke like a native. She sailed through training and was awarded her sky-blue uniform and pin. She was off to exotic locations around the globe and was surely destined to meet all kinds of interesting people.

What did this have to do with me? If I was visiting when Wendy came home from a trip, I got to see all the foreign money she collected. Little bottles of intriguing liquor from drinks service tinkled out of her bag. Best of all, there were presents! My sister and I got sealskin boots from Japan. An "evil eye" necklace from Turkey. A lace mantilla and fan from Spain. Prayer cards from St. Peter's Basilica in Rome. Pistachio nuts from the Middle East. A "slave" ring from Africa. So many treats and trinkets. My mother scolded Wendy and told her she was spoiling us, that we'd only want to see her for what she brought us, but that wasn't true. Her company and the effervescent joy she exuded was enough for me; the rest was icing on the cake.

Our Little Secret

When Wendy was away, my grandmother let me "play" in my aunt's room. I opened her closet and slid hangers slowly along the rack to look at each outfit. I sniffed every phial of perfume. I read the enticing names on each bottle of nail polish. I clomped unsteadily in her collection of high heels and reverently admired each item of her jewelry.

A handled box on the closet floor held her collection of 45s, which I removed one by one and read the song name and artist on both sides. When a record struck my fancy I slipped it out of the paper jacket, then lowered it cautiously onto the spindle of the record player and listened to it.

There was not a single classical recording in the bunch.

I played Ricky Nelson, the Everly Brothers, Patsy Cline, Jan and Dean—delicious, catchy music. When Wendy was getting ready for work she turned on the radio. The station she preferred played music like the Jackie Gleason Orchestra, the Ray Conniff Singers, Johnny Mathis, Steve and Eydie Gourmé and the like—any would have been suitable for my solo party in the bathroom. The only caveat Mom put on my time was that I shouldn't tell Wendy. It was our little secret.

Bambole and Laundry

Sleeping over at Mom's was such a treat. When "the men" (as Mom referred to my uncle and grandfather) left for work, the house was quiet and calm. Mom had chores to keep her occupied and I was left to do pretty much as I pleased. Sometimes I followed her around and we engaged in small talk. Mostly Mom did a quiet whistling under her breath as she dusted or loaded clothes into the washer, which was in the kitchen. Between chores she puffed on a cigarette. Her purse always smelled like tobacco and mints.

On nice days the laundry got hung on a clothesline strung from the brick wall outside the dining room window to a telephone pole on the other end of the yard. Mom, pink foam curlers in her hair, whistled as each wet item got fastened with clothespins and moved down the line via a pulley. The laundry flapped in the breeze, as if greeting all the other laundry hanging on clotheslines down the row of backyards.

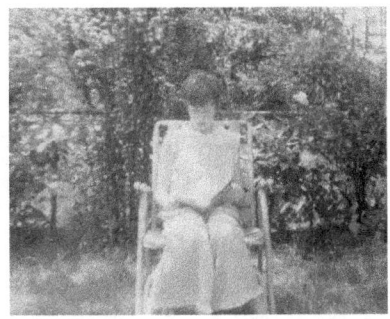
Paula at my grandparents' home on Harding Avenue in the postage-stamp backyard.

The sun shone, the laundry dried, and all seemed right in the world. The washing, hanging, and folding was almost like a ritual. And the smell! Fresh laundry filled the dining room as folded clothing, sheets, and towels piled up on the table.

In the dining room was a china cabinet filled with all kinds of beautiful things—a set of dishes, an ornate soup tureen, a scrolled serving platter, cut glass salt and pepper shakers. My absolute favorite, though, were the bambole—the dolls of Italy that my grandmother collected. If you sent in box tops from packages of pasta (the Prince brand?) they sent one of the dolls in return.

Each doll was five or six inches high, dressed in an embroidered costume, and had a placard with the name of the region or city the doll represented. I lined them up, rearranged them, pleated their skirts, straightened their braids, talked to them in a half-whisper. Eventually they went back into the cabinet, standing patiently, awaiting their next release.

A War Heroine

On one occasion Mom and I were in her bedroom. She said she had something to show me. She opened the bottom drawer of her nightstand and pulled out a small leather box. The hinges creaked slightly as the lid was lifted to display a medal.

Mom told me that during the War she had gone to work for the government, reading international mail since she was fluent not only in Italian but also in French. She was part of a group that discovered the existence of a spy ring reporting the movements of American ships, covertly using the shipment of dolls as a decoy. The ring was followed, arrests ensued, and the spies imprisoned. I was in awe! I felt so proud of Mom in that moment, and still do. I wish to hell I had that medal today; I would display it proudly and honor her legacy as a patriotic American woman.

On the occasions Mom went shopping, I accompanied her. We caught the bus and hit the stores at either the Grand Concourse or Westchester Square. The Square, and the avenues leading up to it, was a marvelous hodgepodge of shops, pizzerias, delis, five-and-dimes (John's Bargain Store was a favorite), bakeries, and clothing shops.

In my mind there is a kaleidoscope. I pick it up. I turn the wheel slowly and, one by one, multi-colored memories slip into place. Prisms tumble by—dolls, nail polish, laundry, buses, cigarette smoke—all saturated with the love and comfort of a grandmother who took this little girl into the home of her heart.

California 1

Come Fly with Me

Since Wendy worked for Pan Am, she was able to get terrific discounts for family members, Paula and me included. The summer of seventh grade, Wendy brought us to California. I distinctly remember the outfit I wore for the plane trip — a navy blue "baby doll" dress with white polka dots and matching bloomer shorts with a white embroidered daisy hem peeking out. I felt too cool, just like a teenager! Flying was not a means of commuting, it was An Event!

Stewardesses (as they were called back then) wore smart uniforms with gold wings pinned on them. They wore hats and white gloves to greet passengers who were no less well-dressed. Women wore chic dresses with stockings and heels; men were dapper in suits, hats, and polished shoes. The cabin was clean with comfortable seats, streak-free windows, and interesting magazines standing at attention in the netted seat backs, ready to be perused.

Wendy proudly wearing her Pan Am uniform.

I squirmed with excitement waiting for takeoff. The engine whined to life, hinting of the might to come. The anticipation was almost overwhelming as the plane turned and made its way to the runway. The engine rumbled from a throaty growl to full-throttled raw power. The pilot increased the RPMs but we weren't moving!

Suddenly, the plane accelerated and we sped forward.

Faster, faster — the dotted white lines on the black tarmac began to blur — faster, faster — my head was pushed ever so slightly into the headrest — faster, faster... and we lifted off the ground!

We arced upward and things on the ground began to get smaller. I wondered, *Will I see my grandparents' house in the Bronx?* Planes were always flying over. No, by the time we were above "civilization" everything was too small to make out individual details. With the insouciance of childhood, the fear of crashing never entered my mind; I was too enthralled with the vibration of the engines, the angle of ascent, the absolute speed and intensity of the machine.

I marveled at the grayness of the landscape below; altitude erased the color and vibrancy of the City. Eventually, when the plane leveled off, I was surprised by the changing scenery as we flew over different regions of the country. There were mountain peaks, bodies of water here and there, pastures striped different shades of green, fields of gold—it was the America Kate Smith sang about. Intermittently we flew above the clouds, which completely obscured the land below. But that was okay because the experience of flying above great mountains of white puffs was exhilarating and my imagination took over. Is this the view angels were blessed with?

After a time the stewardess, in this case my aunt (I was so proud!), came around to take our lunch orders. It was a veritable restaurant in the air! We had a choice of chicken, beef, or salmon. I chose boeuf bourguignon.

While waiting for our food to arrive, Paula and I were treated to a privileged experience. Wendy told us to follow her and we were led into the cockpit. We passengers luxuriated with lounge-type seats and enjoyed plenty of legroom; the captain, co-captain, and navigator were crammed into a ridiculous space, about the size of a closet. One could barely turn around. The amount of buttons and knobs and lights was dizzying. How did they remember what each one was for? I was rendered speechless but did manage to return greetings to the flight crew.

When the meal was served and I got my first peek at lunch, I felt like royalty. Tender cubes of beef were presented in a dark brown, silky gravy, and… mushrooms! This was really living. In my experience mushrooms were the provenance of the wealthy and spoiled. There was no way this could be topped.

But then, a movie was announced!

The crew pulled down screens from the ceiling, fed a large wheel of film into a projector, and hit "play." I don't remember what movie we watched; the fact that I was in the air, satisfied by a French meal, and watching a flick was almost too much to take in. If this had been the beginning and end of the entire experience I would have been content. But there was so much more to come.

Landing was no less exciting, if not a wee bit nerve-wracking. Would the plane slow down enough to meet the ground? Would touching the tarmac be too great a jolt? Would there be enough runway? My fears were allayed and everything went smoothly. Disembarking and getting our luggage was a blur, but meeting Wendy's friend Jim, a handsome, genial man whose hospitality we would enjoy for a week, was a welcome relief from all the hoopla.

Teacups and Whales

Jim lived in a pretty cool house, high up at the edge of a cliff, overlooking the city of Los Angeles. It was the biggest house I had ever been in. He was a nice man but spent little time with Paula and me; his attention was mostly focused on Wendy.

Disneyland with Paula. I am wearing my "baby doll" dress.

We had two excursions planned for the week—Sea World and Disneyland. I had never been to anything like them, since my mother avoided "tourist traps" and only took us to educational venues.

Paula and I spun in teacups. We got splashed chugging on the log flume. We screamed our heads off zipping through the Matterhorn. We ate junk food. We got exhausted. It was a glorious day.

Sea World, of course, wasn't nearly as exciting but fun nonetheless. The Shamu show fascinated me no end. Just imagine, riding on the back of a whale! I had ridden a pony at Belmont Park, and a camel and elephant at the Bronx Zoo, but this was another dimension altogether.

I wished I could fling fish to the whale from the huge bucket. I wished I could play catch with it, tossing a striped beach ball back and forth. I wished I could give it a kiss on its wet, shiny face. Well, I couldn't do any of those things, but I *could* pet the adorable sea otters. Their whiskered faces bobbed up and down in the pool as they flapped their flippers and swam on their backs. They were beggars as they searched for more hands to scratch their bellies. Others were equally entranced and we good-naturedly jostled for positions at the front of the exhibit.

Before I knew it, our week was up and it was time to head home. Since Paula and I were with Wendy, we got to board before anyone else, which was another "royalty" experience!

During the flight I asked Wendy for some paper and a pen; I wanted to write my friend Maureen a letter, telling her all about the trip. There was no lined paper available, so Wendy gave me a placemat from meal service.

I still remember its pale silvery blue with a shiny finish and scalloped edges. I filled the paper front and back, folded it, and put it in my little handbag. When we landed at JFK Airport we went to my grandparents' house, where Wendy lived, instead of going right home.

After all the fuss of homecoming from Mom and Morris, I showed Mom the letter I wrote to Maureen. She read it and quite solemnly asked to keep it. She said it was so beautifully composed. I agreed, and didn't think anything of it. How I wish I had received more encouragement like that—especially from my mother.

Deer Park Elementary

Curlicues and Cruelty

After we moved from West Islip to North Babylon, I started Grade 3 at Deer Park Elementary, now called Marion G. Vedder Elementary, in honor of the woman who was our principal. Our teacher was Miss Roche. She was a sweet young woman with a smooth complexion, dark hair, and smiling eyes. It was in this class that we began to learn cursive handwriting, and I did my very best to emulate the swoops and swirls and curls of the letters printed on the poster that spanned the top of the blackboard. This is where my love of script was born.

I was a shy girl and didn't make any close friends during this year. It was a lonely existence, but I was not at the *very* bottom of the social rung; that place was occupied by Mary Ellen. How ironic that we shared the almost same name. She had short, dark curly hair, like me. Buck teeth were exposed when she spoke, just like me. And she always seemed to have a "deer in the headlights" countenance, like she was perpetually anticipating something bad to happen.

There was a bathroom in the back corner of our classroom, so there was no need to ask permission or to secure a hall pass if one had to "go." When it was obvious that Mary Ellen had to use the bathroom, another student quickly made his way to the bathroom, leaving Mary Ellen to wait. When that student emerged, another again tried to beat Mary Ellen. The poor girl was left in distress more than once.

It was upon this poor unfortunate girl that I attempted to heighten my social standing.

School let out and, as usual, I crossed Deer Park Avenue to walk home. Directly across from the school were two lengths of shops that included the deli that sold sliced round bread (how *did* they do that?) and the laundromat where the infamous Ammonia Sniffing Incident took place. In front of the shops were parking spaces, paved with buckled macadam, and covered with gravel.

Out of the corner of my eye I saw some commotion. Mary Ellen had crossed the road as well, and was on her way home. A couple of boys started chasing her. Aha! This was my chance to be part of the "in" crowd! I started to run after Mary Ellen — what I would do once, if at all, I caught up with her, I had no idea. As I ran, encumbered by schoolbooks awkwardly piled in my arms, I slipped on the gravel and fell to my knees. Oh, the pain! A zig-zagged slice of skin flapped from my kneecap. I bled rivulets down my shin, staining my sock. In despair, I started crying — howling, to be exact.

Some people from the newspaper store ran out and helped me hobble inside. They sat me on a stool at the counter and used napkins to mop up most of the blood. Through sobs and hiccups I cried, "I want my mother!" Of course she wasn't back from work yet, so as soon as my hysterics died down I limped my way home. So much for my career as a hoodlum.

When my mother got home, she cleaned the wound again, over my yowling and protestations, then treated it with mercurochrome and bandaged it. To this day I have an ugly gray scar, a constant reminder of how even the quietest, most innocuous child can easily give in to her worse nature.

I do think of that poor girl from time to time and wonder how her life turned out. Mary Ellen, if by chance you ever read this, I apologize.

That's the Way the Cookie... er... Cake Crumbles

One day Miss Roche announced that we were going to have a bake sale. She instructed us to bring in cupcakes or brownies or cake cut into individual servings. Sadly, my mother was not blessed with cooking or baking skills. Since I didn't know better, it didn't occur to me to have any trepidation about this upcoming event.

The day of the bake sale arrived and after our morning lessons, lunch, and recess, we moved our desks from straight rows into one big U shape, running the perimeter of the classroom. We displayed our goodies and waited for the other classes to come in. Handmade signs in crayon on oaktag paper advertised prices that ranged between five and ten cents.

I excitedly displayed the cake my mother had made. It was in a rectangular baking pan and she had decorated it with her favorite 7-minute icing—which has a marshmallow consistency but with a slight crust on top—and swirls of food dyes and multi-colored sprinkles. If Jackson Pollock and Picasso collaborated on a confection, I imagine it would look like this cake. Since I was used to these "creations," to me it seemed neither outlandish nor weird. Apparently I was alone in that opinion because as kids walked by, perusing each delectable, each conventionally decorated dessert, not one bought a piece of my cake!

If truth be told, a few kids snickered at what graced the top of my desk. I was mortified. A teacher or two must have bought some out of pity because I didn't bring the entire cake home. I felt so badly for my mother. I told her there was so much to choose from that other kids hadn't sold all their baked goods either. That night, after supper, Mommy, Paula, and I ate our fill of the avant-guard concoction, sprinkles sticking to our lips and food dye coloring our tongues.

The Judas Kiss

Finally the last day of school arrived. We gathered the remainders of what was in our desks and made a steady stream out the door. As I waited for my mother to pick me up I saw a few of the girls engage in a cute little ploy. They slyly whispered to Miss Roche, "I want to tell you a secret." As she obligingly bent down, they kissed her on the cheek.

That cunning expression of affection was not in my nature. But ever wanting a sense of belonging, I was prompted to follow suit when my mother arrived. Miss Roche smiled and said thank you in response to my peck on her cheek, but inside I was squirming. I was the child who always hung back, who was reserved. To expose my feelings so publicly was a crack in the shell of self-preservation I had spun about myself.

Even as I bestowed that kiss upon Miss Roche, admiration and affection for my teacher shriveled under the heat of my mother's disapproval—she abhorred falsity. I left clutching random papers and books, head down and eyes firmly fixed on my shoes.

My Heroic Enemy

The ensuing summer involved visits with my grandparents, lots of trips to the beach, and drives to nowhere in particular. My greatest pleasure was to lie on my bed and read. My mother had different ideas. "Get in the car, girls! We'll follow our noses and see where we wind up!" She was big on getting fresh air and exercise. So, inescapably, I found myself in the not-so-great outdoors.

But out in the wide open spaces I was bored! Since it was just my sister and me there was no ball game we could play. No pool to swim in. No net to bat a birdie over. I hated the woods behind my house—bugs and spider webs and rotted leaves and all manner of gross things.

One day, however, my sister coerced me into a game of hide and seek. Jumping over twigs and kicking through dead leaves I inadvertently stomped right on a bee's nest. Instantly my shirt and shorts were covered with swarming, buzzing, angry yellowjackets. I ran screaming out of the woods. They followed me into the yard, where my mother was gardening.

She ran over and started yanking my clothes off, surely getting stung herself. She shepherded me inside and onto my bed. After sponging the emerging welts with a cool washcloth and pulling the sheet over me, she went to the drugstore and bought calamine lotion, which she dabbed on each red bump.

That day, Mommy was my hero.

I was fascinated with our neighbors across the street. There were three houses in a row, each occupied by members of an extended family: Raymond and his parents lived in the first house; Susan, Barbara, and Carol—Raymond's cousins—lived with their parents in the second house; the grandparents lived in the third. They seemed so happy and connected, what I wished for my family.

I liked playing with Raymond and hanging out with his cousins. The girls had fan magazines, and posters of the Beatles on their bedroom walls, and a stack of 45s they played on their record player, while a fragrant sauce simmered on the kitchen stove. I was in awe of them.

In the grandparents' backyard, a long cement patio was shaded by grape vines growing up and around a pergola. Families from all three houses gathered there to share a communal meal, talking over each other in a patchwork of English and Italian. No one cried, or cursed, or pounded the table. Glasses of homemade wine were passed around instead of accusations.

While sitting on our front stoop watching the festivities, someone waved for me to come over and join this domestic *mise en scene.*

I called my mother to the door and told her I was invited across the street. Casting a jaundiced glance, she replied brusquely, "Tell them you have to take a nap." My happy anticipation was crushed under the weight of her disapproval.

I couldn't bring myself to even say the words. I dejectedly waved to the neighbor, turned slowly with hunched shoulders, and went in the house.

That day, Mommy was my enemy.

Comrade Satinoff

School started back up and I was off to fourth grade. I was a quiet, acquiescent girl but inexplicably, my new teacher, Mr. Koechner took an instant dislike to me. As a result I spent a good deal of time standing outside his classroom door in a state of punishment for some perceived offence.

On the first day, Mr. Koechner asked each of us how to pronounce our names. We were then to share about our heritage with the class.

When it was my turn I said, "My name is Ellen Satinoff. It's Russian."

The rest of the year I was known as the communist girl, not the best sobriquet during the Cold War. Predictably, fourth grade became, socially, a repeat of third grade.

One day after recess we lined up to go back to class. A new boy had been added to our room. Andy, the cool, self-proclaimed leader, took the opportunity to introduce us to the newbie. He walked up the row and announced the name of each student.

When he got to me, without offering my name, he said, "We don't like this girl," and punched me as hard as he could in my stomach.

I doubled over and tried to catch my breath, gulping air until the pain subsided. My sight was blurred by tears but I didn't cry. I was too stunned. I straightened up as best I could and waited to get back inside to my seat.

Russian Princesses

Paula has straight hair with a bit of a wave, like our mother's. Mine is curly, like our father's. We both wore it below our shoulders. Getting my hair combed was a tear-inducing event. Every morning the torture commenced; a plastic-toothed comb started at the top of my head and inch by inch was forced through snarls and tangles. When it reached the bottom of one hank of hair, back up to the top it went, my head lolling back and forth on my neck like a bobblehead doll.

"Keep still!" my mother admonished, oblivious to the pain she caused. Paula never made a fuss, so why did I?

Sometimes she let our hair hang naturally, other times in a ponytail. Then, there were the days she braided our hair. Oh, the agony.

She started by making a straight part from temple to nape. One side of the hair was pushed aside while the other side underwent the braiding process.

Sporting the infamous braids.

These were not soft, plump braids that cascaded coquettishly down the back. These started high on the head and were pulled to ultimate tensile strength—UTS, defined as the maximum stress a material can withstand while being stretched.

As the braid was being formed, skin on the forehead strained as tight as a drumhead. A vein popped out and began throbbing. Most often a headache ensued.

The result was a braid on each side of the head that stuck out at an awkward angle, like it had suffered a compound fracture. But none of this—or our complaints—deterred Mommy.

"There!" she exalted as she stepped back to admire her work. "Doesn't that feel so nice, off your face and neck!"

This procedure was traumatizing enough. But the final indignity came when the braids were loosed and a zig-zag of waves were released. We looked like the products of a home perm gone horribly wrong. But not to Mommy.

"My two Russian princesses!" she gushed, hands clasped to chest. In her mind we mirrored the beautiful, doomed daughters of Tsar Nicholas and Tsarina Alexandra.

In my mind we just looked weird.

Russian princesses posed on the settee, with my cat Susan.

Miss Carmody

There was nothing soft about Miss Carmody, the Assistant Principal; she was all elbows and knobby knees. A pale woman with violent red hair, She was short and slightly stooped, vertebrae protruding through her fussy blouses and cardigans. Glasses hung from a chain around her neck and she seemed to permanently be holding a stack of papers.

Her physical appearance belied her personality, however. Miss Carmody was kind and never raised her voice. She also became my sister's "best friend." Paula was often in her own little world, full of imaginary beings and happier landscapes. But she was—is!—brilliant. She was just a square peg teachers were trying to pound into a round hole. As a result, she was often sent to the principal's office.

Paula wasn't rowdy or disobedient. I think the teachers just didn't know what to do with her. But Miss Carmody did. She let Paula follow her around and they engaged in their little conversations. For all I know, Miss Carmody saw herself in Paula and totally "got" her. My mother used to get called in for the dreaded parent-teacher meeting about these incidents but I think eventually everyone gave up and the status remained quo.

At some point Miss Carmody went to the hospital for an operation. Mr. Koechner said it would be a nice gesture to make get well cards to be delivered to her. Construction paper and crayons were distributed and we went to work.

The girls all came up with the usual clichéd ideas, decorated with hearts and birds and flowers. The boys mostly wrote "Get Well Soon" in big block letters. Except for Kevin. He was a clown and stereotypically sported freckles and blazing red hair, but unlike Miss Carmody was round and plump. Mr. Koechner ambled up and down the rows of desks to observe our work. When he got to Kevin's, in a disdainful tone he told Kevin his card was "*not* appropriate" and ordered him to make a new one.

I had seen Kevin's card and I thought it was hysterical. On the front he drew an empty hospital gurney. Miss Carmody was running after it, yelling, "Hey, wait for me!" The height of fourth-grade humor. I felt bad for Kevin, who, to his credit, didn't seem particularly bothered, and for Miss Carmody who probably would have appreciated it.

The Unthinkable

One day we had a substitute teacher, Mrs. Leakey. Her daughter, Deborah, was in our class. As we trooped back from lunch we saw Mrs. Leakey sitting atop the teacher's desk, legs crossed; she had on black high heels. Her face was pale and she looked disturbingly serious. After we were seated she told us, gently, that President Kennedy had been shot and taken to the hospital.

A pall of silence fell over the room. I don't think we knew how to react.

When I got home my mother was already there. Every TV station was carrying the news that President Kennedy had died. One of our elderly neighbors, an Irish woman with an honest-to-goodness brogue, didn't have her own television set and came over to watch on ours. Rocking back and forth, she was keening and carrying on. My mother turned the TV off and said, "That's enough." She firmly escorted our neighbor to the front door, concerned this overwrought display would further upset Paula and me.

The next days brought the Jack Ruby shooting of Oswald, headlines in thick bold letters, and somber newscasters replaying the events: Jackie in her black veil, John-John saluting his father's casket, Caroline in a short coat wearing shoes that matched her brother's, horses clopping down Pennsylvania Avenue pulling a casket. It was a very confusing time.

Kate Smith and Cigarettes

My fifth-grade teacher was Mr. Conroy, my favorite teacher of all time. Each day started out with the Pledge of Allegiance and the morning prayer, streamed over the loudspeaker. A different student was chosen to read the announcements each day—a great and coveted honor.

Mr. Conroy went the extra mile, though; he had a small record player behind his desk, and after the Pledge and prayer, a 45 blared out Kate Smith singing "God Bless America," and per Mr. Conroy's direction, we sang along.

He made a contest out of it; who was going to sing better, Kate or us? Of course we wanted to be winners so we chirped out the anthem as well as we could. Yelling or screaming was not allowed—decorum was not sacrificed in this endeavor.

Mr. Conroy regularly moved student desks according to our deportment, and it was a privilege to be in the back of the classroom because that meant you didn't need the teacher watching you. He did cool things like demonstrate the health hazard of smoking by actually *lighting a cigarette in the classroom,* and blowing the smoke through a white handkerchief to show us the brown stain it left.

A visionary, he predicted that by the time we became adults, roads would move the cars along instead of cars driving on the road. He also told us that by the age of 18 some of the boys would be fighting in a place called Viet Nam, but I didn't believe that.

Pickles and Eggs in Ancient Egypt

One of the projects we were assigned was to make a timeline of ancient history. Mr. Conroy broke us up into groups each of which was responsible for a certain period. We were to make this a pictorial history on poster board, to be tacked up on the walls going all around the room. I was assigned to the ancient Egypt group.

I was very excited! Ancient Egypt was so exotic. Mommy had taken us to the mummy exhibit at the Museum of Natural History and my mind was swirling with ideas: headdresses adorned with golden asps; kohl rimmed eyes; sacred, mystical cats.

There was just one problem: I was not an artist.

My mother was pretty good with paints and colored pencils so I went to her for advice. She told me "pickles and eggs." Everything could be drawn using the shape of either a pickle or an egg—since heads are smaller they could be eggs, and limbs are longer so they could be drawn using pickle shapes. That made sense to me and I went to work.

On the due date I brought my poster to school and shared it with my group. They were aghast. They laughed. They said it was unacceptable. Even Mr. Conroy seemed annoyed and assigned one of the others in the group to redo my portion.

I was humiliated and angry with my mother. Why couldn't she have drawn the outline for me and I could fill it in? She was probably trying to encourage me to do it on my own, or maybe she recognized my lack of talent and was trying to simplify it for me.

In any event, I think it was a case of displaced anger—anger at myself for not doing better, anger for being the object of ridicule by the other kids, anger for Mr. Conroy's insensitive dismissal of what I had created.

Mr. Conroy was my hero and I felt betrayed. The outward me, the me everyone saw, rolled up in a ball of embarrassment and tried to make myself as unobtrusive as possible. *Don't get noticed. Hide inside yourself so no one sees you. Look down.*

But inside I was screaming. I was seething. I was confused and searching in every possible direction to try to understand what was wrong with me. Why could I not make friends? Why did other kids make fun of me? Why did I have to walk home from school alone and have boys shoot spitballs at me? Why couldn't I be normal like everyone else? Why did I have to have curly hair when every other girl's hair was straight and silky and shiny? Yes, I was angry and had no place to put all that emotion.

I soon found a place.

The Big F

Each of us had access to a stack of dictionaries kept in the classroom. One day, bored, I was leafing through my dictionary. With no preplanning or formulated intention, I took a pen and wrote "FUCK" at the top of one of the pages. In capital letters. Then I wrote over it and over it until it stood out and could not be unnoticed. The page was etched with my rage.

Where had I heard that word? Even my grandfather, who could swear like a sailor, never uttered that vile expression. At the end of the lesson I returned the dictionary to the stack.

A few days later one of my classmates went up to Mr. Conroy, carrying an open dictionary. The two spoke in muted tones and the boy returned to his desk emptyhanded. I watched Mr. Conroy open a drawer and retrieve a pair of scissors. He cut out a small piece from the top of the book. I felt ashamed, but also triumphant. *I bet he'd never guess who wrote that*, I crowed inwardly. In one word—just four short letters—I caused my hero to vandalize a book. But deep down I knew what I had done was wrong and shameful. I wished I could take it back.

Finally Made it to the Top

Sixth grade arrived and hurray! We were the top dogs in the school. Mr. Lankenau and I had a mutual ambivalence toward each other— I think he felt there were more interesting kids in the class, and as far as I was concerned nobody could meet Mr. Conroy's exalted status.

Every day we had a period of quiet time, during which we could read whatever we pleased. Mr. Lankenau meandered in and out of the rows of desks, checking out our books and making occasional observations. One day he came to my desk and turned my book over to read the title. It was *Exodus*, by Leon Uris, an epic saga of the rebirth of the land of Israel that dealt with some very adult situations and relationships.

"Does your mother know you're reading this?" he inquired with incredulity.

I looked up, baffled. "She *gave* it to me."

He stood there digesting what I'd told him, and then moved on.

Exodus detailed the horrors of the Holocaust, the travails and experiences of the characters, the struggles of the early settlers in Israel. It also formed the basis of understanding of my Jewish heritage.

I was an 11-year-old girl who sill played with dolls (I actually named one of my dolls after a character in *Exodus*) and watched cartoons. I could also orchestrate the destruction of school property; words exerted a powerful influence over my life, albeit subliminally. These two identities were not able to coalesce and added to my already confused sense of self.

So I'm a Drug Addict

Occasionally there were assemblies, but this one was unusual in that only grade six attended. Seated in the back of the assembly hall, I was only able to see the stage if I bobbed back and forth between the heads in front of me. Mrs. Vedder gave a short speech and then introduced the special guest.

This guy came out dressed in bell-bottom jeans (gasp!) and a striped tee shirt. He had longish curly hair. Our attention was immediately riveted. This was most decidedly not the usual type of speaker. He was here to talk to us about drugs and drug addiction, topics of which I was totally ignorant. I didn't know what they were called, what they did, where you got them, or what they looked like.

He talked about sticking needles in his arms and being homeless. He talked about getting beat up. He talked about how he had craved drugs until they were all he thought about. This is when my attention waned. His voice receded into the background as the realization slowly and horrifically dawned on me… I was a drug addict!

I had in my pocket a box of honey-flavored Pine Bros. cough drops. I ate them like candy whether I had a sore throat or not. I could feel the box burning a hole through the pocket of my sweater. I tried not to think about them but I wanted one so badly. I wanted to feel my molars satisfactorily sinking into the delicious soft drop. I wanted to feel it slowly melt as I rolled it from one side of my mouth to the other. Oh, this was torture! I gave in and put one in my mouth. I felt ashamed for not being able to resist. I was a weak, pathetic, helpless addict!

After this realization the worries started piling on: would I wind up homeless? Get beat up? What would my family think?

I was brought back to reality by the applause that broke out. The assembly was over. We marched back to class. "Walk in a straight line! No talking!"

For the rest of the day I worried over my woeful situation but by the next morning thoughts of my doomed life disappeared. Something more disturbing loomed in my immediate future.

Blood and Milk

One Saturday my mother reached for something in the refrigerator and in the process knocked into a glass milk bottle which promptly crashed to the floor and broke. She tried to catch it but gashed her hand severely, right in the fleshy part between thumb and forefinger. There was blood everywhere. It mixed with the milk in a revolting pinkish swirl. It dripped down the refrigerator door. It puddled on the floor. I panicked as my mother's lifeblood pulsed out of her.

She wrapped a kitchen towel around her hand and calmly walked next door. She asked Mrs. Sabatini to stay with my sister and me while she went to the hospital. As I watched my mother drive away—never to be seen alive again, I was sure—Mrs. Sabatini cleaned up the mess. When I came into the kitchen, practically hysterical, Mrs. Sabatini did her best to console me, but she didn't understand the depth of my fear.

What if my mother died? I had no father—where would we go? My grandmother was so good to us, but all I had ever heard was what a terrible mother she had been, and how abusive and hateful my grandfather was. Every time my mother and grandparents were together there was screaming and crying and yelling and castigating. Is that what my life would become?

Until my mother arrived back home, left hand bandaged like a mummy (inconveniently, since she was left-handed), I was inconsolable. The upshot of all this is that I didn't get my homework done that night.

The next day I confessed my omission to Mr. Lankenau. As I started to explain what happened, he dismissed me with a wave of his hand and a barely disguised air of disgust. I was both crushed and angry. Didn't he understand how traumatic this had been for me? Hadn't he noticed my wavering voice? My trembling lower lip? In all fairness, though, he probably thought, *So her mother cut her hand. What's the big deal? Just an excuse to get out of doing homework.*

Surely Mr. Conroy would have understood.

I Saved the Day!

It was a hot summer afternoon in June (air conditioning in school was unheard of in those days) and Mr. Lankenau promised us an extra recess IF someone answered a question correctly. We had been studying the Revolutionary and Civil Wars. Mr. Lankenau said slavery had been an issue even during the Revolutionary period but it hadn't been addressed until the Civil War.

His question was, why wasn't the fight to end slavery taken up *before or during* the Revolutionary War? He gave us ONE MINUTE to come up with an answer.

There was dead silence.

Kids stole glances at one another, silently begging someone to figure this out. Come on! An extra recess was riding on this! The second hand on the wall clock tick, tick, ticked our hopes away. Twenty seconds left! Suddenly, a hand shot up. My hand! Mr. Lankenau pointed to me.

"Because if we didn't fight the Revolutionary War then *we* would be slaves of *England*," I answered. "We had to be free first and then we could fight for everyone else's rights."

The answer had come to me like a bolt out of the blue. It was so obvious! The class actually erupted in cheers. I felt so proud… I had saved the day and for one shining moment, I was a hero.

Broadway Babies

As was tradition, we sixth graders were to put on a play. A musical. A gala affair, with costumes and plenty of scenery. Written by our music teacher, it featured some popular songs. Two songs I remember were "Anything You Can Do, I Can Do Better," and "If I Ruled the World." The setting was in South America and my role was as a drum majorette. I think somehow the Peace Corps was involved. How all these elements came together to make a cohesive story is a good question. In any event, part of the play consisted of a number of students chosen to give a brief overview of each South American country. Mine was Nicaragua.

My costume was red, white, and blue, fashioned out of a slippery, silky material, and included a cape. My mother's ability to sew was eclipsed only by her inability to bake. Therefore, this was going to be a problem. Fortunately, my uncle Bobby's girlfriend Shirley had a sewing machine *and* the requisite skill.

The director was our music teacher, Mr. Hudson, a portly man with oily black hair. He sat on a squeaky stool that struggled to support his girth, as did his shirt buttons. He was a kindly man, however, and we kids liked him.

As practice, we performed the play for the rest of the school. The Main Event would be held during the evening for parents and other family members.

After supper we performers reassembled at the school. We changed into our costumes and gathered backstage. Oh, the nerves! Last-minute costume adjustments. Rehearsing lines. A final comb through our hair. Whispers. Jumpy stomachs. This was it—cued by the piano, the curtain slowly rose.

Everything went swimmingly until, during a pause in the music, a voice from the back shouted out, "This play is shit!" A gasp went up from the audience. Those on stage stopped dead in their tracks, unsure of how to proceed. This kind of language was never bandied about in public. This was scandalous! Mr. Hudson deflated like a balloon, and I will never forget the look of sorrow—yes, sorrow—on his face.

After a stunned silence, Mr. Hudson came back to himself and the play resumed. The perpetrator was the older brother of a new student. He had a dubious reputation, which after this incident, was cemented. Happily, that was just a blip on an otherwise perfect evening, and we received many curtain calls to sustained clapping.

Two weeks later we were graduates of elementary school! Junior high awaited us and I felt quite intimidated by the prospect.

I didn't have long to dwell on the coming September as my mother announced we were going camping, and for practically a whole month!

On the Road

Hitchin' a Ride

My mother possessed an insatiable appetite for daring and adventure. Back in the early 1950s she persuaded her aunt, Louise, to go hitchhiking from Manhattan to Boston. Louise was demure, a timid soul who had a distinct sense of propriety. The fact that my mother could convince Louise to be a partner in such an escapade speaks to Mommy's peerless powers of persuasion.

So they rolled up their denim pants, slipped their bobby-soxed feet into loafers, tied kerchiefs on their heads, filled two backpacks, and set out. On the road they were picked up by a trucker. They sat in the front seat of the cab and all seemed to be going well until the driver's hand wandered from the gear shift to Louise's knee.

My mother most certainly was not going to put up with this behavior and decided to beat a retreat. Luckily, she was sitting on the far outside of the passenger seat, which allowed her to open the door, hook her arm through Louise's, and hurl the two of them out of the truck.

North by Northeast

Fast forward to the late 1960s, and the travel bug bit again. Mommy decided on a less dangerous but equally audacious venture. We were going to go camping! She and her friend Alyce—who was as madcap as my mother—planned the trip down to the last detail.

At Sears & Roebuck, which had an extensive outdoors department, my mother purchased a tent that slept ten. Add to that, sleeping bags for herself, my sister and me, a Coleman stove, enameled pots and pans, a camping percolator, plates and place settings, a lantern, suitcases, and a storage unit for the top of the car.

A car! We needed something more reliable than the one she had driven to Boston, so off to the dealer she went. She bought a Chevy

Biscayne which she swore had been "built around a dead rat," since it had a slightly foul odor we could never get rid of. The car was gleaming white with a cheery red interior and a trunk the size of a studio apartment. The final purchase was a Super 8 camera, intended to record our trip for all posterity.

Alyce was, like my mother, a kindergarten teacher. She was loud, and funny, and matched my mother in zaniness. She also fancied herself glamorous. Think Carol Channing crossed with Marilyn Monroe. She had four children—two boys and two girls—three of whom accompanied us. (The older boy was 16 and considered this trip way below his threshold of coolness.)

Mommy and Alyce bought maps and spent several afternoons plotting highways and side roads, and selecting campgrounds. The plan was to head north with the first extended stopover in Maine's Acadia National Park and then on to Canada. Prince Edward Island was the northernmost goal but as it turned out we instead went to Nova Scotia.

The women packed the car: suitcases stacked in the trunk along with the stove, pots, and pans. Items were shoved into the canvas rooftop carrier. Folded sleeping bags laid across the floor of the backseat where we girls—Paula, Alyce's two daughters Valerie and Marjorie, and I—were assigned to sit. Alyce and her son Don were up front and my mother, who, never one to cede control, was behind the wheel.

Unbelievably, we all had enough space. But it was hot. Rolled-down windows offered the only, albeit noisy, relief. Fortunately, our first stop was only three hours away, where we emerged sweaty, slightly grumpy, but excited to officially begin our adventure.

Submarines and Whale Teeth

Our first stop was Mystic Seaport, the oldest maritime museum in the country. To me, it was just a bunch of old boats bobbing up and down with the swells of the water slapping the sides of the dock. Shops with fake antique gold-lettered signs — "Ye Olde" whatever — sold weird things like whale teeth. My mother and Alyce were enthralled with all the historical plaques and buildings, but I was bored.

Wait — what's this? Tour a submarine? That's more like it. We walked down the short wharf to a decommissioned sub, and were helped onboard by a (quite cute!) sailor. My mother had the Super 8 camera ready to go, and I can still see the film of myself descending the ladder into the bowels of the vessel. I was wearing a dress that pouffed out when the breeze blew under it (thinking back to church, I was worried about the sailors down below looking up my dress) and had a matching scarf tied on my head. Inside it was disappointingly dark and dank and I couldn't wait to get out.

After the submarine, we walked through a small museum that was filled with ship wheels, ropes (what could possibly be interesting about rope?), shark teeth, black and white photos, oil lanterns, and scrimshaw.

To my relief we were finally finished with all Mystic had to offer and headed on to our next port of call, Sturbridge Village in Massachusetts.

The Bad Old Days

Sturbridge Village was a working community that replicated life in the 1700s. Horses left evidence of having clomped along dirt roads, which hosted peppered clouds of black, buzzing flies. Nevertheless, curiosity in what was taking place in each of the structures along our route mostly overshadowed any discomfort we felt. The heat (and the smell of horses!) was discouraging — do we *have to* tour the entire village? — but we pressed on, and were rewarded.

My favorite exhibit was the pottery shed. *Whap!* A lump of wet clay was slapped on the wheel, like the potter held some unresolved grudge against it. But slowly he shaped his forgiveness into the contour of a mug. No, wait… his remorse lifted the squat mug into a graceful vase, like a ballerina on pointe, resolving any residual tension between creator and creation. The final product was then slid gently into the kiln, where their mutual and lasting symbiosis baked into a permanently fixed union. I saw so much beauty and poignancy in this peaceful, solitary art.

By contrast, the blacksmith hammered and beat glowing, angry iron with clanging raw power, forging the resistant metal into a serviceable tool. This was the artistry of a heavyweight prizefighter, determined to pummel his opponent into submission. Spirals of acrid smoke spewed out of the fire in protest of each new object shoved into its center. A barrel of water hissed as red hot material was plunged into it. Pitchforks, wheel rims, children's hoops, and ax heads were lined up alongside key rings and window locks. Large or small, none could withstand the smith's muscle and might.

Candle makers, broom weavers, seamstresses, pewterers, farmers, and even musicians all worked in harmony toward a common goal — the enrichment and success of the community. In the middle of this hive of activity a white clapboard church stood silent, surveying the affairs of its communicants, a still, sure beacon of blessing on all their endeavors.

Hot, sweaty, and dusty, we hopped on the splintery sideboard of a wagon pulled by a team of yoked horses who trudged along in plodding resignation. What a relief to be able to sit down! We passed a field of wildflowers that swayed like a church choir to the music of the breeze. Farmers in black pants and straw hats plowed fields.

Children ran up and down a crossroad, each beating a hoop with a rod, trying their best to keep it from corkscrewing to the ground. Bonneted women in floral dresses that dragged in the dust strode purposefully with baskets, some towel covered. And so, passing along through bucolic tranquility, we reached our goal. We hopped off the sideboard and followed the scent to the door of the bakery.

Up two granite steps and we were inside, eagerly waiting our turn to buy gingerbread cookies and lemonade. Fine dust from our clothing floated to the creaky planks of floorboard. Finally, we stood at the front of the counter. A bonneted lady with red cheeks and moist skin handed us a paper sack and cups. Warm, spicy cookies and tart, cool lemonade were the reward for our long afternoon in the summer sun.

Of course, no attraction is without a gift shop and Sturbridge did not disappoint. For the kids there were dolls, candy, and all kinds of geegaws that entertained the children of bygone days. The adults were offered more serious items: racks of cloth in old-fashioned prints, area rugs, furniture, decorative pieces, and books.

Since our car was already at full capacity, my mother limited herself to a small box of maple candy—to which she became immediately addicted—and a pair of bayberry candles. On her many subsequent trips to New England she replenished her stock of candy and candles.

Because we were only going to be in Massachusetts for one night, we left all our camping gear in the car and rented rooms in a country inn. Suitably quaint, it perfectly complemented the day's experience. New England-style quilts adorned the beds. A braided rug covered the floor. The scent of pine wafted through gingham-graced windows. After viewing lumpy straw-filled mattresses and chamber pots, I was thankful to be back in the modern world.

The next morning greeted us with promise; puffs of white clouds dotted blue skies and a pleasant breeze wafted through the pines. It was perfect weather for flying down the highway unhampered by foul weather—we were finally on our way to the "Maine" event, Acadia National Park. And since my mother didn't feel we had accomplished anything unless we drove a grueling 500 miles a day, I guess we got to Acadia pretty quickly.

A Clown Car and Hobo Ham

Having arrived at Acadia National Park we took our place in a line of cars that snaked its way to the Ranger's post. When we finally got our entry pass, we drove slowly along a narrow route that meandered in and out of the pine forest and eventually became a dirt road that led to the campsite. We got to our assigned lot and my mother cautiously backed into the parking area. Then the disembarkation commenced.

The process looked not unlike cars at the circus, where an impossible number of clowns keep spilling out. My mother, Alyce, Don, Valerie, Marjorie, Paula, and I tumbled out on legs wobbly from being cramped in the car for hours.

Out came sleeping bags, suitcases, pots and pans, pillows, cardboard boxes with foodstuffs, and The Mighty Tent.

First order of business was to get the tent erected. This was no small feat; a bag of metal rods was emptied of its contents in a jangling pile and then the canvas was unrolled flat on the ground. Diagrams were consulted and poles were inserted in the appropriate slots and then connected to each other. With much heaving and ho-ing, grunting and groaning, the tent was lifted to the sky—a canvas cathedral in this heavenly woodland setting that became our magnificent home for the next two weeks.

Like rustic congregants, other campers had assembled to watch the proceedings. Not only were we a spectacle, but the fact that all this was being coordinated and accomplished by two *women* was nothing short of astounding.

The tent erected on our campsite in Acadia National Park.

My mother and Alyce were not teachers for nothing—everyone had their assigned spot in the tent. We kids scurried like ants to unroll our sleeping bags and put our belongings neatly next to them. (It's amazing we didn't have roll call each morning.)

Naturally after all the driving and unpacking we were starved. In addition to our camp stove, there was a pit in the ground with a cooking grate over it. My mother got a fire going and when the embers were deemed the right color and heat, a ham was placed on the rack. A glaze of maple syrup, mustard, and spices was slathered over the meat. The smell was divine. People walking by commented on it and my mother generously offered each spectator a sliver. Hobo Ham, she called it, and it was a great success.

Barron's in the Pines

The days were filled with nature walks, climbing rocks, reading, dipping our toes in the icy northern Atlantic, shooing away mosquitoes, playing cards, making up stories, stoking fires, and the occasional bickering between kids. This is when I learned Mommy had decided I would not be attending Deer Park Junior High School, but instead was to be enrolled at The Academy of Saint Joseph in Brentwood.

As she constantly reminded me, this was a highly demanding, accelerated educational program where the *crème de la crème* attended. In preparation, she had brought along Barron's books — thick educational practice books separated by subject; tests were in the front and answer keys in the back. The series was created for kids to study for the Regents exams.

The Regents diploma was a coveted document for those planning on college after high school. The State of New York issued them to students who scored a minimum of 65 percent on the Regents exams in each subject. My mother was determined that I must ace the exams because, as she relentlessly repeated, I was now competing against the Top Minds in the State. No pressure, then.

So each day, while the other kids cavorted, I spent part of the morning wrestling torturous word problems in math (never my forte), vocabulary definitions (my favorite), confounding topics in science (is that an amoeba or a paramecium?), history (loved it), and every other conceivable subject designed to torment an 11 year old.

A Crustacean Education

One cannot vacation in Maine without indulging in lobster, and we were no exception. My mother and Alyce had scoped out several "lobster shacks" and picked one for us at which to lunch. Whereas in

New York people queued up in the bakery or the deli, here we lined up for our turn to order crustaceans.

Just as one pointed to a particular babka or specialty salad, we were told to indicate the lobster we wanted. We quickly learned that the bigger (older) lobsters had more meat but the smaller (younger) lobsters were sweeter.

We sat at a warped, weatherworn picnic table right next to the ocean and watched fishing boats bobble up and down in the water. We smelled the salt in the air. We saw steam clouds rising to the sky from the bubbling lobster pots. And now here came our dinners — brilliant red lobsters splayed on paper plates with little ribbed containers of melted butter, a mound of coleslaw, a sweet roll, nutcrackers and picks, and lots of napkins.

Except for Alyce, none of us had ever tackled an entire lobster before, so she schooled us on proper procedure. We each sat engrossed in our own little world as we pried jointed legs apart and sucked out the meat, cracked open the claws to reveal beautiful white meat, and then attacked the motherlode, the tail. Butter dribbled from our chins and hot seawater dripped down our fingers. Slurping abounded — manners be damned! This experience cemented Maine as my favorite state, right behind New York.

Conquering the Cliffs

In Acadia there is a rock formation known as Otter Cliffs, which I didn't understand since I never spied a single otter. They are flat, broad rocks bordering on a cove of the ocean. This was a favorite spot for rock climbers, and my mother determined that we were going to conquer it. One by one all we kids scampered across fissures, dug our fingers into crevices, pushed up with our legs, and felt quite Olympian.

All, that is, except me.

I was petrified. I imagined myself losing hold and sliding mercilessly down the cliff, flayed by rough stone, and drowned in the Atlantic.

I clung to the granite with all my might. The sight of the ocean below, beating the rocks with eternal, predatory patience, terrified me.

"Sssss," the roiling foam hissed, taunting me. *"Fall in and I will carry you out to the briny wasteland."*

"Come on!" my mother encouraged. "It's such fun!"

She had brought me from the safety of our campsite, ringed with a protective stand of titan Maine pines, to this terror. I watched other children scamper over the cliffs like nimble, gleeful sea-creatures playing hooky. Some were as red as the lobsters they would surely eat at the evening's meal.

I, on the other hand, was pale from secluding myself in our canvas haven. Uncomfortable in this wonderful wilderness, I preferred to escape into a book. But my mother decided this was the day for me to venture forth and conquer fear of the rock, fear of the ocean, fear of fear.

"Come *on*," my mother urged.

I resolutely shook my head.

"I'll help you," she reassured.

She crab-walked across the face of rock until she was about two feet away from me.

"Here," she held out her palm. "Skootch over this way and take my hand. You're doing great! Put your foot in that crevice. Now move sideways."

With wobbly weak-kneed steps I inched my way toward her, not daring to look down. She wiggled her fingers by way of enticement. In a step of faith I reached out and grabbed Mommy's hand. She held on to me the rest of the way and we successfully reached the other side.

I wondered inwardly why it was so important to climb these rocks. What purpose could this ever serve? The sun made me squint, etching lines on my face that foretold future worries. My shaking, sneaker-covered toe found the crevice. I moved sideways and then upward. Inch by barnacled inch I made my way to the top, exhausted from the sheer climb, the sheer terror.

I was drained… and amazed. I looked down, down at the ocean. The sun set off sparks as it struck the surface of the water. Bobbers marked lobster traps on the sandy ocean bottom, waiting in inanimate indifference for their unsuspecting prey. In the not-too-far distance the yachts of those who would never need to learn rock-climbing swelled and fell with a complacent rhythm. My legs still shook but I suddenly felt exhilarated. I breathed in the piney, salty air.

"See?" Mommy smiled. "It wasn't that hard."

I was so surprised at my accomplishment that I didn't know what to say. Timorously I made my way back to where I had started. Pushing aside apprehension I went back across the rock path again, solo. I became the Edmund Hillary of the Cliffs. From that day forward, each time we went to Otter Cliffs I couldn't wait to climb the rocks.

I had trusted my mother and she had not let me down.

Bologna in the Biscayne

After two weeks we packed up our campsite and drove to Nova Scotia. Well, we drove to the *ferry* to get to Nova Scotia. Thankfully this trip did not mirror our crossing to Boston so no seasickness was involved. After the journey we waited as our car was unloaded and then we were on our way to a new campsite.

My mother navigated to a beautiful area and we picked a site right off a lake. Once again the car was unpacked, the tent erected, and our beds laid out.

The sky grew gray.

My mother and Alyce assembled the items for supper.

The sky grew grayer.

I was lying on my sleeping bag, reading, when the first clap of thunder let loose. My mother called us kids to gather at the picnic table, out of the tent held up by metal poles. Rain appeared as if Zeus had opened the sky and emptied buckets of water one after the other. Angry waves rolled across the surface of the lake. (I had no idea lakes could produce waves.) Another peal of thunder exploded.

"Everyone get in the car!" my mother barked, pointing to the vehicle in case we had forgotten where it was.

We raced across drenched grass and launched ourselves inside. Even though it was mid-afternoon the sky turned black. The air was a weird combination of gray and yellow and smelled like ozone. We watched through the rainstorm as best we could and were treated to a display of power by Mother Nature that we had never before witnessed.

Bolts of lightning hit the water and sizzled across its surface, sounding like steak on a hot grill. It was terrifying and awesome at the same time. The windows fogged up from our collective breaths. It was apparent we weren't going anywhere any time soon.

Ever the planners, my mother and Alyce had scrapped whatever the dinner plans had been and instead had collected bologna, bread, mayonnaise, and a knife, which Alyce stored in the glove compartment. After the shock of the storm wore off, we kids started complaining.

"Get off my seat!"

"Your feet stink. Put your shoes back on!"

"I'm thirsty."

"When is this going to be over?"

"Will the car explode if lightning hits it?"

In the wisdom of all mothers, Mommy and Alyce decided that in order to shut us up we should be fed.

As the door to the glove compartment banged down, Alyce announced ceremoniously, "The kitchen is open!"

She slathered mayonnaise on bread and slapped bologna between the slices. As the last sandwich was made she slammed the glove compartment shut and declared, "The kitchen is closed!"

We chewed our bologna sandwiches, occasionally wiping fog off the windows to watch the majesty of the storm. At last it abated. Convinced that it was well and truly over, my mother and Alyce let us escape from the confines of the car.

Upon returning to the tent we discovered to our dismay that, naturally, everything was soaked. Our tent was big and roomy, but it was not waterproof. Sleeping bags were soggy. Pillows smelled of damp. A random drip plinked from the roof. A newly formed streamlet rippled under the floor. This was going to be a very uncomfortable night.

After a wet, restless evening we awoke to a beautiful morning, as if the day before had been a cruel dream. Things were still wet but the blue sky and sunshine promised better things to come.

Not surprisingly, that did not include a campside breakfast. The box of pancake mix was sodden and the seats of the picnic bench swelled from saturation. The adults were not in the mood to cook and no one was eager to sit on the wet benches. So off to town we went, where we found a cheery café bedecked with checkered curtains.

Thankful for what promised to be a delicious meal, we made our way to a booth. Naturally, the first thing Mommy and Alyce ordered was coffee. I had long ago learned to look at the right hand of the menu first, where the prices were listed, and to pick the least expensive item. But this morning my mother magnanimously ordered a full breakfast for herself, Paula, and me, which included an item called Canadian bacon. It was a rare treat after a night of terror and bologna sandwiches.

Ambrosia it Ain't

Ever since this trip was first formulated in my mother's mind, she had told Paula and me about Canadian bacon. The superiority of Canadian bacon. The yumminess of Canadian bacon. Wait until we get a taste of Canadian bacon! My mouth was primed and salivating. I waited impatiently for my food to be served.

At last! Our waitress made her way to our table, balancing our breakfasts on a tray—plates with golden eggs, buttered toast, and… what the…? Where was this manna? This extraordinary slice of gustatorial goodness? This epicurean miracle? I saw nothing resembling bacon. Instead there was a round piece of ham plopped next to the eggs. Well this was unquestionably the biggest letdown. I had never been so disappointed in my life. What a sham!

I don't know if my mother had only read about Canadian bacon's unparalleled gourmet properties and had elevated it in her mind to be as the ambrosia of Greek mythology. In any event, I could not have been more deflated. Now if I see Canadian bacon on a menu, I actually laugh out loud.

While we were at the café we learned that some locals had lost barns overnight, along with other properties and even cows. Turns out it was the worst weather incident to have hit that area in 75 years. I was pretty impressed that we had withstood such a storm, adjacent to a lake, eating bologna in the Biscayne.

Bay of Fundy

The next spot on our itinerary was the Bay of Fundy, famous for its tidal range, the highest in the world. This didn't exactly sound thrilling to me, but after the letdown involving Canadian bacon I figured things could only go up from there.

When we arrived the tide was out. What lay before us was a wide, empty bed of mud. Brown, oozy mud. Paula, remembering our experience at Sturbridge, decided we should become potters. We ventured out into the riverbed. The muck slurped our feet into its depth like suction cups. We collected pails full of mud that we laboriously hauled back to shore. As we upended the buckets onto a picnic table, the contents leached out in blobs. We worked to fashion little bowls, and even one ashtray, to be given to our grandmother. Mommy kindly let us lay our creations on the back dashboard of the car to dry and harden, which they eventually did. She kept one as a cherished memento, right up until her death.

As we were lining up our pottery in the car, someone yelled, "It's coming! It's coming!" Paula and I scrambled outside and ran to the bank.

Straining our necks to follow where people were pointing, we could just make out a white line that stretched across the riverbed, moving in our direction. At first I didn't understand what I was seeing. A line in the water? Moving? Then it dawned on me — this was actually the tide, and it was rolling in with a vengeance! No gentle laps like when the ocean sneaks up the sand, little by little, so that you don't notice until the towel you're lying on gets wet. No, this was a relentless, determined advance of the river, and it was a magnificent thing to behold. Even I, so indifferent to the wonders of nature, was forced to admit this display of energy and power was mighty spectacular.

Back to Home Base

Now that we had seen and experienced all we had set out to, it was time to head home. My mother approached this challenge with the gravitas of an astronaut returning to earth from space. No more sightseeing. No little villages off the main road to explore. Nope, this was pedal to the metal time, and none of it to be wasted. Bathroom stops only when absolutely necessary. Lunch again served out of the glove compartment. We made it from Canada to Boston in one shot and stayed somewhere unremarkable overnight. The next morning we hastily gulped down bowls of cereal and hit the road. We made it back to the Island the next afternoon.

After dropping Alyce and her kids at their home we made a beeline for ours. Unencumbered by four extra people—and all their apparatus—the Chevy practically grew wings and flew us to our house in North Babylon. Paula and I begrudgingly helped to unload the car (had we really packed all this stuff?) and were released to go to our room. Sneakers and socks were stripped off hastily and we flopped on our beds. Aah… our own mattresses! And here came my cat, Susan, purring as loud as I'd ever heard her and twining herself around my legs.

Home.

The Academy

Dressed, but Not to Kill

Summer was coming to an end and I faced the prospect of seventh grade at The Academy of St. Joseph. This was not your average Catholic school. Situated on 200 acres of prime Long Island real estate, it housed the juniorate, novitiate, convent, retirement home, and nursing home for the nuns. The school accommodated both day students and boarders. I, of course, was a day student.

Many of the borders were from foreign countries and had fathers who worked in embassies or the United Nations. It was not unusual to see these girls deposited from shiny black limousines boasting diplomatic plates. Most day students came from affluent families. Horseback riding and tennis lessons were available, and in addition to the traditional classroom subjects, instruction in ballroom dancing was mandatory.

Social and economic status notwithstanding, the school strove to enforce uniformity. Literally. Our winter uniforms consisted of pleated wool skirts and vests buttoned over white blouses with Peter Pan collars, a navy blue blazer, and the ugliest shoes imaginable. The skirts were to reach just below the knee but as soon as we were released for the day they were rolled up to mid-thigh.

As seventh graders, and newly blossoming "young ladies," we were expected to wear stockings (pantyhose were a thing of the future). To save money on stockings, which easily got "runs" just looking at them, my mother decided I should wear the sturdier support hose. To compound this indignity, they were not held up by a sexy garter belt; every morning I had to struggle into a girdle that surely was constructed of cast iron.

We wore blue uniforms from the first through the 15th of the month and then switched to our green uniforms. This was to allow time at the dry cleaner's. Failure to wear the correct color incurred a fine.

Any time we left the school for trips we also donned black velvet tams and white gloves. Propriety and decorum were to be studiously observed and those nuns meant business.

In the spring we switched to warm weather uniforms—a shirtdress that featured a flared skirt and matching belt. We were free to choose from a variety of pastel shades, so that we were a gaggle of greens, pinks, blues, and yellows. White dresses were reserved for Holy Days of Obligation.

As miserable as I had been in elementary school, I was now, if possible, more so. Despite the nuns' best efforts, the economic divide was great, as was the social one. A girl from a modest Cape Cod home simply could not compete with those from the understated snooty elegance of the Upper West Side of Manhattan.

Thanksgiving perfectly illustrated the fiscal disparity. Sister Paul Francis decided we would bless a needy family with a holiday meal. She asked us for menu suggestions whereupon the blackboard quickly filled up with all manner of gourmet goodies. Sister brought us to sobering reality, though, as she tallied up an approximate cost; would our allowances be ample enough to furnish such a fabulous repast? Where could we cut corners without cutting the quality? Thinking back to Thanksgivings at home (meaning when we didn't go to our grandparents') I thought I had the perfect solution.

"Instead of buying a whole turkey we could get a turkey roll that comes in a box," I offered.

Sister frowned disapprovingly.

"We should never give something that is any less than we would have ourselves," she admonished. Harshly.

I slumped down in my seat. After her reaction there was no way to explain that we, indeed, had eaten boxed turkey. I felt ashamed at my situation and angry at Sister for assuming that I was being cheap.

The Breakfast of Champions

Happily, I did make a couple of friends. Karen lived in the same town as me, and Maureen came from a family of eight kids. Karen and I saw each other occasionally outside of school but I had never been invited to Maureen's house, nor she to mine.

I had one sleepover at a girl named Ginny's house. Her mother was a doctor or scientist. Ginny was extremely bright, and her mother was hospitable in an absent-minded way. Did we play games? Watch TV? Go outside? The only thing I *do* remember was that we had to scavenge for breakfast ourselves, which ultimately consisted of chocolate chip cookies and V8 juice. Our mothers probably would have gotten along like a house on fire.

Spoon Fed

Since Brentwood was several towns away I took the bus to school. As in Queens, we arose early to get ready for its arrival. The nuns really piled on the homework, which meant late nights for me. I was perpetually tired. Every morning was a struggle to get out of bed and dash around in preparation. Where's my other stocking—I can only find one! How did this math paper get a rip in it? What day is it, blue or green? Only 10 minutes until the bus gets here!

Breakfast was a rush job. Sometimes my mother had pancakes ready, which I didn't like. I would chew, chew, chew until there was just a gluey glob in my mouth, which I tried to swallow with a gulp of milk. I didn't like milk. Eggs were fine, scrambled or over easy. But some mornings, the dreaded bowl of oatmeal awaited. I felt like Oliver Twist confronted with a bowl of gray, gloppy gruel. One morning my mother was so disgusted with my reluctance to eat it that she sat in front of me, spoon in hand, and commanded me to open my mouth. I gagged at the pasty mess. I don't know which was worse, the actual oatmeal or the humiliation of being force fed at age 12.

There Will Be Nun of That

The uniforms were itchy wool. The nights were an unending mountain of homework. Mornings were a blur of confusion. But none of this compared to the fear I felt of the nuns.

We had two teachers. Sister Michelle Marie taught English and history, and Sister Paul Francis, who taught math and science. I enjoyed history and excelled at English (diagramming sentences is fun!). Science was manageable but math was just beyond me. It was a constant struggle.

Sister Paul Francis didn't believe it.

I worked as hard as possible, practically suffering an ulcer in the process. I had always been prone to stomach issues, but this brought them to a whole new level. Assignment after assignment and test after test came back with failing grades. Sister accused me of failing on purpose, of not studying, of being willfully recalcitrant. Finally, she threw me "out" of the class, which meant banishment to the back of the classroom by myself when it was math time. When my mother came in for the parent/teacher conference, Sister told her I made faces at her during class! (Why didn't Mommy ask her what I was doing in the back of the room?) I didn't "make faces." I wouldn't have dared!

I was probably trying not to cry.

I suffered through seventh grade, and then through eighth, and then my mother decided we were leaving New York for good.

My eighth grade class

My eighth grade graduation picture

On the Road... Again

Florida Bound

The summer of seventh grade was our second camping trip. This time we were headed south—final destination, Florida. Again, the car was packed (we were pros by this point) but only for six; Alyce's son Don decided he was too old to be traipsing around the country with a bunch of females. This was fine with us girls since it meant more room in the car and less care when dressing.

Our first planned stop was Gettysburg, Pennsylvania. We set up camp and stayed for a few days, making the obligatory tours of the battlefields. As we drove through town we passed a hardware store that advertised, in big white painted letters, "FERTERLIZER." Alyce got the biggest kick out of that and her raucous laugh filled the car for a full five minutes. She would say "ferterlizer" and then howl all over again. The sign was funny but her reaction was funnier.

Gettysburg was noteworthy in that it was the last time we were to enjoy sunny weather on the entire trip.

The Steamy, Stormy Smoky Mountains

The midway point, and the supposed highlight of the adventure, was to pitch camp and tour the Smoky Mountains. To enjoy the area's full splendor, Mommy and Alyce forewent the usual bare-boned KOA (Kampgrounds of America) campground and instead splurged on a site in the Great Smoky Mountains National Park. They paid the entrance fee and we began the arduous task of finding an open spot.

But wait! What's this? A perfect location! Flat, no rocks, shaded by towering pines and oaks, and plenty big to accommodate our tent and gear. Mommy and Alyce couldn't believe their great good fortune in stumbling upon such a picture-perfect place. Mommy backed the car (still the stinky Biscayne) off to the side and we scrambled out onto a soft, spongy bed of pine needles. 1-2-3 and the campsite was set up. In acclimating ourselves we noticed that across the road there was a very steep hill with a well-worn path. Too late, we were informed by a group strolling by that this was where bears often made their nighttime trek down the mountain to peruse what "goodies" they could find. The hikers thought we were so brave to pitch camp here.

Sometimes ignorance is not bliss.

Mommy, Marjorie, Paula, Valerie, and Alyce.

Rain and Pancakes

That first night we did not sleep well. Every little noise made us jump, anticipating the arrival of bears. Mommy had taken great care to secure all our food but even so we were not reassured. At one point during the night both Mommy and Alyce needed to visit the restroom. They slipped into their sneakers and Alyce grabbed the kerosene lamp. As a defense, Mommy grabbed a blue-speckled enamel pot and a metal serving spoon, and the two of them clanged their way to and from the bathrooms. I wonder if the other campers were impressed with their life-saving tactics. Once they returned, and order was restored, we did nod off. Happily, nothing in our site was disturbed. Unhappily, the following day it began to rain.

A lot.

Mommy and Alyce, troopers that they were, decided the rain couldn't last forever. We would stick it out, have breakfast, and hope for the clouds to pass. Alyce put on a pot of coffee and we miserable kids stayed in the tent. Mommy donned her raincoat, which was a sight in itself. It was a thick plastic affair, almost floor length, just brushing the tops of her sneakers. The sickly pinkish color of Silly Putty, it didn't have a hood, necessitating the need for a hat, which she clapped on her head.

Standing under the canopy of the tent entrance, which sagged perilously from the accumulated water, she began to mix a batch of pancakes.

As she stirred the batter, she was puzzled that it didn't thicken at all. Actually, it was downright watery. Finally, she figured it out. Instead of pouring reconstituted powdered milk into the batter she had been adding plain water. Stepping out of the (relative) protection of the canopy, she poured the whole mess on the ground and started over. Needless to say, breakfast was a miserable affair.

At last, reluctantly, Mommy and Alyce had to declare "uncle." It was obvious that the rain was not even close to abating. Everything we had was drenched. There was no respite in the tent. We couldn't get warm in the damp sleeping bags. It was time to admit defeat and head south.

We returned all our gear to the car and deconstructed the tent. This was to be a real challenge, since it was made of thick canvas. Heavy at the best of times, soaking wet it was almost unmanageable. Somehow, Mommy and Alyce got it down, and the poles disengaged, but there was no stuffing it back into the storage bag. So they folded it with about as much finesse as one does a recalcitrant fitted bedsheet, and using every ounce of muscle wrestled it into the trunk of the car.

The Smoky Mountains turned out to be a bust. Mere mortals cannot compete with Zeus so we set our sights on Georgia.

A Rocky Experience

There was no redeeming the soggy tent so when we reached the Peach State, Mommy and Alyce selected a motel and registered us. Lawd a' Mighty, we kids were stoked! Real beds, an in-room bathroom, and… a pool! Not one of us mourned the tent. We had lunch at a modest little diner and headed back to the motel.

The day was picture perfect, which meant we could go swimming. We eagerly switched into bathing suits and plunged into the blessed blue water.

Except Paula. She walked the perimeter of the pool, studying the white rocks that bordered the concrete pad. Her swimming attire looked odd. My mother noticed.

"Paula, what are you doing? Come and get in the water with us. Wait… what's wrong with your bathing suit?"

Mommy hoisted herself out of the water and went over to examine. Her mouth dropped open and her eyes widened. Now we were all intrigued and hung onto the sides of the pool to watch the drama unfold.

My mother reached into Paula's bathing suit and dropped something on the pad. It made a dull thud.

"What's going on over there?" Alyce wanted to know. We all wanted to know.

Apparently, Paula had wanted to see how long she could stay under water. She figured filling her suit with rocks would help reduce her buoyancy.

That's Paula for you.

Florida, Finally

The next day, after breakfast, we loaded our suitcases in the car and took off for our final destination, St. Augustine. The weather gods weren't finished amusing themselves at our expense, so rain once again poured down as we left Georgia. After an interminable five-hour drive we passed the border into Florida, windshield wipers waving furiously. An outsized billboard appeared down the road. As we approached, my mother leaned far over the steering wheel and squinted to make out the message.

Suddenly she hooted uproariously. "Welcome to Florida, the Sunshine State," she read out to us. As if on cue, we all burst into laughter — the irony was blatant.

Once again we checked into a motel and spent the night in relative comfort. Upon waking, my mother opened the drapes and glory be! The billboard was right! The sun was out, the sky was blue, and it promised to be a beautiful day. Mommy and Alyce declared it was safe, weather-wise, to venture out and explore. We fished bathing suits out of our suitcases and headed for the beach. The water was calm and palm trees waved lazily. Mommy and Alyce dragged the sodden tent out of the trunk of the car and laid it out on the beach to dry.

As day turned to dusk, the tent was reloaded and we reluctantly headed to our motel. So far, this had been the best — and most uneventful — experience of the trip.

The following day we made our way to St. Augustine, the oldest continuously inhabited city in the United States. It had the feel of a town, and was almost obscenely full of history, Spanish architecture, and enviable homes. But the heat and humidity! I was torn between fascination and downright misery. However, both the natural and manmade beauty stemmed my grumpiness and, all in all, I have to say the day was a success.

Well, the tent was dry but since it had lain out on the beach it was now also gritty. Instead of canvas the tent seemed to be constructed of sandpaper.

I hoped the accumulated debacles of this trip would put an end to our camping adventures.

Alas, that was not to be the case.

Leaving, Not on a Jet Plane

This Thing is Not Like the Other

Our final camping trip was a one-way venture but the telling of it is circuitous.

In 1968 my mother decided she wanted to move out of New York to get away from her parents, a decision she came to every few years but heretofore had never acted on. Crucial to this story is the death of my grandparents' dog, Duke. Of course they were heartbroken — Duke really was an exceptional animal. Every night, when he decided it was time to go to bed, he snuck up to my grandparents' room and pulled down the covers on their bed, apparently as carefully as a maid in a 5-star hotel. He never got caught doing it… until one day he did. Chagrinned to having been found out he never pulled them down again. Anyway, as sadly happens with all pets, he passed away and my mother decided Mom and Morris needed another dog to get over their grief.

Mommy found a Bassett hound puppy for sale and named her Hildegard. She had droopy eyes that reminded my mother of Marlene Dietrich, hence the German name. The great day came and we delivered Hildegard to her new home in the Bronx.

Previous to said delivery, my mother told Paula and me that she planned to move us to Colorado. This news was delivered with the strictest of instruction that we were *not, under any circumstances*, to tell my grandparents. Paula and I were sworn to secrecy. So, off we went to bring Hildegard to Harding Avenue.

Needless to say, my grandparents were stunned when we arrived with this squirming, sad-eyed puppy. And not in a good way. They didn't really say anything — I think they were too shocked — and the visit went off without, for once, any confrontation.

Not surprisingly, my grandparents did not want this dog. They called my mother to tell her so, and to request the name of the breeder in order to return her. This of course, did end in a confrontation. The same old back and forth.

(My mother) "Nothing I ever did was good enough for you! I never could please you!"

(My grandmother) "You never consider anyone else! You can be so thoughtless! You didn't even ask if we wanted another dog!"

(My mother, now half screaming, half sobbing) "I try and try but it's never enough! You never even wanted me anyway! You never loved me!"

(My grandmother, now sobbing herself) "I did want you but you never let us love you!"

Etc., etc., etc.

On and on, ad nauseum.

How, you may ask, do I know both ends of the conversation? Simple. These accusations, these pleadings, occurred every time my mother and grandparents got together, with all the heart-wrenching, hand-wringing, torturous table-pounding and screaming you can imagine.

Anyway, the upshot was that my mother gave up the phone number for the breeder, who subsequently offered to come and retrieve the cause of the uproar. And now you will know what the puppy had to do with us moving to Colorado. When the breeder arrived at my grandparents' house, he off-handedly commented on how they would be missing their grandchildren once they moved.

This conversation I was not privy to, but I can imagine the aftereffect was one of shock, despair, and then anger. I was feeling distraught myself, knowing that I was going to be so far away from my grandparents, especially Mom, and sailing off into the Great Unknown.

My mother plowed ahead with her plan. She gave (gave!) the house and all its contents to her brother Bobby, who was only too happy with this windfall. We simply took our clothes, records, photos, books, and my cat Susan. We would camp our way cross country, accompanied by my mother's trusty travel camping buddy, Alyce.

It's Really Happening

The day arrived when we were to depart. Bobby stood at the door of his newly acquired property and said goodbye as we trooped out, one by one. I was the last to leave. Clutching Susan in one arm, the other encircled his neck and I hugged him as tightly as I could. I loved him so much! He hugged me back and unceremoniously told me to be good. I hoped his seeming indifference masked a sense of loss as deep as mine.

We drove over to Alyce's house and then hit the road for good. It was when we were on the highway that I asked my mother what plan was in place if we got to Colorado and didn't like it. "We'll just keep going to California," she responded breezily, as if picking out a state to live in was of no more importance than selecting a new toothbrush . The State of Colorado? The State of California? The state of confusion? Doesn't matter, one is as good as the other; it's all just a grand adventure. I, on the other hand, was apprehensive and in actual anguish over what awaited us in the Great West.

During our trip, there were two momentous occurrences. The first took place in Ohio. We camped only one night. (No keeping my mother from reaching her goal! She was on a mission.) In the morning, as Mommy and Alyce were packing up, I looked for my cat, Susan. She was nowhere to be found. I walked around a bunch of other campsites, calling her.

Sadly, my mother said we had to leave but she did drive around to look for her. We drove slowly, calling her name, but to no avail. After about half an hour my mother said it was a lost cause. I was heartbroken. Completely bereft. I loved that cat; she had been my companion for years. Inwardly panicking I imagined all manner of disaster to befall her. It was one of the worst days of my life.

The second incident took place in Kansas. Not as dramatic as a tornado, but scary just the same. We had upgraded from a tent to a pop-up camper—smaller, lighter, and much easier to assemble. Upon our arrival at the KOA we went about the now-familiar routine of setting up. The pop-up popped up, sleeping bags laid out on our respective areas (Mommy and Alyce on one side, Paula and me on the other), kitchen area organized. We spent the late afternoon stretching and relaxing from the long ride while Mommy prepared supper.

We ate and cleaned up. The sun set and the stars came out. The campfire was doused, and it was time for bed. Sleeping contentedly in the dark velvet hours of nighttime, we were abruptly awakened by a bang and a great shuddering. Was it an earthquake? A tornado? (Visions of Dorothy and Toto flying by.) We shimmied out of our sleeping bags and attempted to make it out of the pop-up.

It was like trying to dismount a tilt-a-whirl that was in full tilt. We spilled over each other to get outside and expected to see all manner of mayhem. Thus, we were surprised to discover that everything around us was… as it should be! The entire campground was quiet and intact, but we were as disheveled as carnival clowns, nightclothes askew and hair scruffy from sleep.

Surveying our site it became apparent what had happened. One of the pop-up's aluminum poles had bent and then collapsed. Since my mother's side was heavier it flopped to the ground like a dying canvas fish, while Paula's and my side, seemingly defying gravity, bobbled up in the air, swaying like a cart at the top of a Ferris wheel.

The four of us let out a collective sigh. Paula and I stood aside while Mommy and Alyce mended the pole as best they could. After much clanging and banging—and the occasional swear word—we cautiously reentered the disabled camper and eventually fell back to sleep.

The next morning we folded up the camper and reattached it to the tow hitch. The carnival was over and we four gypsies hit the road.

Well, We Made It

As we neared Colorado, I became more depressed and disoriented. The barren terrain was bereft of landmarks to which I could anchor myself. Tumbleweeds blew by the car, as aimless and adrift as I felt. Where were the towns? The parks? The highways? This was a foreign country and I was an alien.

Irritatingly, my mother prattled on about the beauty of natural land, the blueness of the sky. The independent spirit of long-dead explorers seeped into her pores. She waxed poetic. I closed my eyes and longed for the sound of traffic, of an airplane, of anything to assure me I was not lost.

Eventually we arrived in Colorado Springs. Since it met Mommy's approval she found us an apartment on the outskirts of the city (city—hah!) in a small complex that was still under construction. Our unit had two bedrooms, a small eat-in kitchen, a living room, and one bathroom. My mother was ecstatic that we had a panoramic view of Pike's Peak, rising to a majestic height. I longed for the sight of a skyscraper.

Eager to explore our new State, Pike's Peak was one of the first places we visited. My mother was determined to make the ascent by car; she was not afraid of the drive and shunned the tour bus. So with her at the helm, Alyce in the navigator's seat, and Paula and me in the back (sans seatbelts), off we went. Round and up and round and up and round… oh my God—a tour bus was coming straight at us. My mother slammed on the brakes and the car responded by stalling.

Stalling and sliding.

As in sliding toward the sheer drop at the side of the road. (Guardrails? Of course not.) My heart beat at an unnaturally high rate. Mommy got the car restarted and gunned the accelerator. The tortured Biscayne (still stinky but admirably dependable) proceeded onward and upward.

"Well, *that* was exciting!" she chortled.

I was liking Colorado less and less.

After we were relatively settled in our new digs, Alyce flew back home to Long Island. It was one of the few times I saw my mother cry that was not connected to going rounds with her parents.

Or maybe it was.

Being in a completely new place, without employment, with only the company of two dependent girls, she must have felt overwhelmed in that moment.

Sometimes even Mommies need their mommies.

Meeting New People

I liked our apartment in the newly constructed complex. It was the right size for the three of us. Everything in it was contemporary, and I liked the fact that there would be a lot of other people living around us. Also, the construction crew foreman, Dave, was really cute. My mother struck up a friendship with him and his wife (darn!) Julie; I even babysat for them a few times. They had a little boy three years old and an infant. Both parents were 20, their youth being unremarkable; a couple of girls in my freshman class actually already sported tiny engagement rings!

Dave and Julie invited us to dinner for a summer meal. The baby was in his crib for nap and, as babies will, started crying. Nobody went to check on him because babies cry, right? Except he didn't stop. Neither parent made a move. The unrelenting wailing seemed to intensify and was torturous to hear.

Unable to stand it any longer, Mommy got up to check on him. I was embarrassed; why did she always have to butt in on other people's business? But we all followed and traipsed to the nursery.

There was the baby, red in the face, with his head stuck between two slats of the crib. It was a horrible sight. His mother extricated him and he eventually calmed down, but the whole experience was incredibly unnerving. I knew how he felt — stuck, caught, and unable to free myself.

I was a prisoner in the wide open spaces of Colorado.

Another dinner with Dave and Julie was shared at our apartment. After the meal the adults sat around the table talking while Paula and I went into our bedroom. Returning to the living room I heard my mother wrap up (what to her was) an amusing anecdote.

As previously mentioned, I had read the book *Exodus*. One passage described in detail a scene of foreplay between the two protagonists. At the time, I found it repulsive and unfathomable. Why did the woman allow the man to do such a thing? (Remember, I was only 11.) Subsequently, I told my mother that if any man tried to do that to me I would kill him. My mother thought that was uproarious. Funny enough to share with this couple that we only knew a short while.

The room closed in around me. Unobserved, I slunk back to my room. My cheeks burned. My heart pounded. I ground my teeth and punched my palm with my fist. I was furious and felt utterly betrayed. *"Why?"* I screamed internally. I felt murderous and if I'd had a knife I would have slashed my bedding, attacked the wall until the blade snapped. My mother had no right to make me the butt of her story to garner attention. Why did she never protect me, even in her storytelling?

Bowed over in a defeated stance, I held onto the windowsill for support and lifted my eyes to look through the pane. The sun was setting, and streaked the sky with a red that was as heated and angry as my heart.

A Blazing Birthday

Mommy made friends with a fellow teacher. Florence was round and soft, and wore dresses that were from another era, but not in a good way. Her hair was short and had been subjected to many a home permanent. Cat's eye glasses perched on the bridge of her nose, ever so slightly off kilter.

She was a divorcée and lived in a small house with her son and aged mother. The son was pudgy and wore pants whose waistband sat above his paunch of a belly. He was a boy who would grow into a man sporting thick-rimmed glasses and a pocket protector, never to be invited to after-work drinks. Florence's mom, unlike her daughter, was reedy, with a network of blue veins running up and down her arms and a halo of poufy white cotton-candy hair.

One evening we went to Florence's to help celebrate her mother's birthday. We had a simple supper and then cleared the table for the celebratory confection. Florence lit the candles, put the cake at her mother's place, and returned to the kitchen for forks and plates. My mother was also in the kitchen. I sat at the table as the birthday girl shuffled in pink quilted slippers to a chair and proceeded to sit down.

The process evolved thusly: she pulled out the chair and hobbled to the front of it. Slowly, slowly she bent at the waist to lower her bottom to the seat. As she doubled over she leaned farther and farther above the table.

Over the lit candles.

And then it happened.

She was directly above the cake when her hair caught fire. Completely unaware, she finally made it to the seat, halo sizzling on her head. I was aghast but—horror of horrors!—started laughing. The whole thing was so absurd. I managed to sputter out a terrified "Mommy!" in between belly laughs.

My mother poked her head in, took one look, and charged into the dining room, kitchen towel in hand. She covered the blazing head and smothered the flames. The smell of burning hair was dreadful. Florence bustled to her mother and fussed over her mightily. Mommy gave me a look that told me I was in store for some serious consequences when we got home.

I don't know why I laughed. That poor old woman was so confused (thankfully she hadn't been hurt) and the outcome might have been much worse. Maybe I was relieved to meet someone who was as helpless as I felt. Or maybe it was terror at what might have happened. But it was the first good, hearty laugh since we took up Colorado residence and it felt cathartic.

Old Ladies and a Drunk

We had arrived in mid-summer so naturally school was not in session. It followed, then, that I knew absolutely no one. It dawned on my mother that I was bereft of a circle of peers, something she had never noticed before. She decided to remedy this and immediately took action.

So off we went into "the city" to the YWCA, which offered a wide array of courses for teens—tennis, volleyball, swimming, dance. I was looking over my mother's shoulder, perusing the roster, when she suddenly made her choice.

"Golf!" she enthused.

The lady behind the counter jumped slightly and came closer to assist us.

"What about golf?" Mommy asked me. "You'll be outdoors, you'll get to walk... You like to walk, right?"

As she jabbered on about the many merits of the game—of which she knew nothing—her voice morphed into warped, unintelligible sounds as I cringed at this latest prospect of humiliation. What made her think I had any interest in golf? I tried to imagine myself in skorts and cleated shoes, lugging a bag of clanking clubs that weighed who knows how much... sweating, huffing with effort, squinting in the damned desert sun... No, nothing about this appealed to me at all. By the time I came out of my trance, however, my fate was decided as my mother had already paid for the course.

The first day of lessons arrived. In shorts, sneakers, and deodorant I eased out of the car, heat waves swirling up from the macadam and twining around my feet.

Please don't let any of the other girls be too good, I prayed, in hopes that my lack of skill wouldn't be made immediately apparent.

We signed in and somehow I found a golf club in my hand. We were directed to a grassy area some short distance away and Mommy waxed quite rhapsodically at how wonderful this all was. Look at the blue of that sky! Oh, those mountains are the perfect backdrop! And the grass! I've never seen such green grass! On and on as we approached the small group that... had... gathered...

Hey! What the heck? It was a bunch of old ladies! They turned and smiled at my mother, sunlight spangling off their silver hair. "Hi!" they greeted her. They came toward us, clucking like a hatch of chickens. A little belatedly my mother realized they thought *she* was the new student. She disabused them of their mistake when she introduced me as her daughter, who was here to take lessons. Suddenly I had a clutch of new grandmothers. They fussed over me, suffocating me with their welcoming.

"Well, I can tell you're in good hands, Ellen," my mother assured me. "I'll see you in an hour!"

As our little group scratched and pecked, eagerly awaiting our instructor (except for one of us, guess who), one of the women noticed a figure tripping toward us.

"Laaaadies!" a man's voice trilled.

We looked up and saw a silhouette, his features obscured by the intense rays of the sun blazing upon him. He greeted us and then introduced himself as our instructor.

He talks funny, I thought.

He herded our little assembly somewhat further out onto the grass, tripping once on the way. I inspected the ground carefully, determined not to make the same mistake. Once we reached our destination he began to expound on the virtuous qualities of the game and the personal growth to be experienced just by stepping onto the turf.

"Golf is a lifelong quest for perfection and redemption," he preached.

I wondered at which point we should genuflect.

He carried on with his little sermon, occasionally stumbling over his words.

Geez, I thought. *First I'm stuck with a bunch of old ladies and now I get a teacher with a speech impediment*, thereby affirming my conviction that this was a game for losers.

Our first lesson consisted of instruction on how to properly stand and hold the club. As we hunched over our imaginary golf balls the teacher made his way around to each one of us, straightening an elbow here, adjusting a stance there. Eventually it was my turn to be inspected. He came up behind me to adjust my stance and then all the little things I had noticed made sense.

The man smelled like a distillery.

He was a drunk! I almost had to laugh. Here I was, a 12-year-old girl with a bunch of crones, ostensibly learning to play a game I had no interest in, being taught by an inebriate, in order to "make friends." I felt like a character in a Samuel Beckett play. Not surprisingly, there were only a few more lessons and then we were informed that the remainder of the course had been cancelled. Apparently our instructor needed "time off." I could not have been happier.

Mine Shafts and Donkey Meat

Over the summer Mommy invited our great-aunt Louise to visit. To my amazement, she actually agreed to come! This from a woman who mostly lived in her own little neighborhood in Manhattan and never ventured out of New York. But she bought a ticket, got herself to the airport, and flew out to Colorado Springs. I was so eager to see her, a familiar face and a piece of New York. I think my mother was feeling lonely and isolated, too, and was glad for the company.

Mommy was keen to show off our new home. We drove here and there—eschewing another trip up Pike's Peak; we were now content to admire it from afar.

My mother was itching to tour Cripple Creek, a former gold mining town. In its heyday, Cripple Creek was quite the bustling burg, thanks to the many men who were drawn there by its promise of wealth. Inevitably, women arrived and for a while it looked like the prosperous towns depicted in TV westerns of the '50s. When we got there, however, it was a sad, ramshackle ghost town.

Hardly anyone lived there and the amenities were few; it was a broken down, dusty shadow of its former glory. The most it had going for it was a mine that visitors toured, descending to the bowels of the earth, to experience what it was like to be a miner.

Mommy decided we should do this. So we bought our admission tickets and stepped into a precariously rickety contraption that evidently was supposed to be an elevator. I had my doubts. Louise didn't look convinced either. But as the metal gate clanged shut we put on miner's helmets and brave faces, and slowly dropped into the dark.

Although I was scared, it was kind of thrilling, sliding down into the unknown. Thankfully, the temperature was the only thing that fell. At the end of the descent we squeezed our way out of the box and marveled at the scene.

We were in a dark, almost airless tunnel that snaked out of view. The walls were constructed of packed earth and dotted sporadically with lanterns. Empty coal carts stood ready to make their way to the next vein and be filled with the earth's booty. The tour guide offered facts and anecdotes, all of which are now buried in the tunnels of my mind.

Eventually it was time to leave and we jostled for space on the wobbly elevator. At the surface we blinked against the abrupt blinding light. *What would this life have been like*, I wondered. Did any of the miners ever get claustrophobia? Did anyone lose an arm or leg to a pickax? Could they get black lung from mining gold? It was my own private moment of reflection and these were sobering questions to contemplate.

I wasn't to be reflective for long, however, as Louise complained of being hungry. My mother immediately sprang into action, looking up and down the dusty, unpaved street. "Mom's Café," Mommy read a sign hanging over a cute little building. We walked toward the door and I saw the requisite red and white café curtains on brass rods in a broad window. It was clean inside, and charming.

I suddenly realized I was hungry too. I envisioned sitting in front of a platter heaped with sliced meat, brown gravy puddling around it, and mashed potatoes, and maybe some buttery corn. My mouth watered. We tumbled in, hot and sweaty and ready for something cold to drink.

The waitress, a sweet young girl, handed us menus. After a short review, we all ordered the roast beef platter. We sipped iced colas ("pop" in the local vernacular) and took stock of the other patrons. They seemed to be tourists as well.

The adults sat opposite Paula and me. Louise was squished next to the paneled wall. Our meals arrived. I dug in like a starved miner!

I started eating and sadly, the taste did not live up to my dream. The meat was dry and stringy, and instead of a delectable brown color the gravy was more… gray. I was disappointed but decided I was hungry enough to keep eating.

My mother took a bite.

She made a face.

She took another bite.

She put her fork down.

"Stop eating," she ordered us.

I looked at my mother and saw That Look on her face.

She turned this way and that, searching for the waitress, and when Mommy caught her eye, called her over.

Innocent and unsuspecting, the sweet young thing complied.

"We ordered the roast beef platters," my mother declared. "What is this?"

"That's our roast beef platter, ma'am," the waitress replied proudly.

Louise stared down at her plate. My head went back and forth at the exchange between my mother and the waitress as if I were watching a tennis match. Paula started to take another bite.

"I said put that down," my mother commanded.

Paula's fork clattered onto the plate. A splotch of gravy struck the tabletop.

My mother then held up a piece of meat between her thumb and first finger as if it were something diseased. Gravy dripped off it, congealing into an irregular blob on the plate.

Louise's shoulders shook ever so slightly. I realized she was trying to hide her giggles.

"This is *not* roast beef," my mother stated. "This… is… *donkey meat*. I recognize it by the fur!"

Her voice became louder and more determined with each syllable.

Louise was holding her napkin up to her mouth. She had tears in her eyes and was rocking back and forth. I never saw anyone laugh so heartily without making a sound. I was afraid she might explode.

I felt sorry for this simple girl who had never encountered the force of nature that was Mommy.

"Let me check with my manager," she stammered as she backed away from our table. Maybe she was afraid to turn her back on us.

When she returned she told my mother that we didn't have to pay for our meals and then she actually apologized. People out west were so polite.

We got up from the table and left Mom's Café, much to the relief, I am sure, of the waitress, the other patrons, and "Mom" herself.

A Rootin' Tootin' Good Time

Our next big adventure with Louise was an outdoor meal at the Garden of the Gods, a national treasure boasting impressive rock formations against the "backdrop of Pike's Peak" (is there no getting away from it?) and original home of the Red Rock People and other indigenous tribes.

The menu was barbeque, of course, put on by some civic organization. We arrived to find a large covered pavilion with lots of picnic tables. Quite a crowd had gathered and we hurried to claim seats.

The air held a savory aroma and I was eager to eat. I had never had real barbeque; I'd had grilled hamburgers and hot dogs, and the occasional piece of steak, but this was real Western-style barbeque with pulled meat in a tangy sauce. The smell was so pungent I believed I actually tasted it before it was served.

Once everyone arrived and all the tables filled we were instructed to line up, grab a plate and utensils, and move on up the chow line. Soon my plate was filled with barbeque, corn bread, baked beans, and coleslaw. I managed to hold it in one hand and a paper cup of lemonade in the other.

After we were all seated and diggin' in (don't I sound like a real cowgirl?) the entertainment began. It was music by none other than the Sons of the Pioneers, who, in their earliest incarnation, featured Roy Rogers. It was a yodeling good time. They played their hit "Tumblin' Tumbleweeds" and other songs they were famous for. Between tunes they told stories and jokes and a good time was had by all.

The day came when Louise was to fly back home, and I think she was sad to leave us but also kind of relieved.

There's only so much yodeling and donkey meat a city girl can tolerate.

But Yes, We Have No... Roaches

One afternoon I came home from school and to my surprise Mommy was already there. She was on a stepstool and all the kitchen cabinets were emptied. Plates and canned goods and small appliances were taking up space on every counter and table surface. The place smelled horrible.

Apparently my mother had spied a roach and went into full New York tenement mode. She was *not* having roaches in her home. Roach paste had been smeared into every seam of each cabinet, and the coup de grace, a choking cloud of Raid was covering all the sides and backboards of each cupboard. Those roaches had no idea whom they were up against.

I swear, from that day forward, every bowl of cold cereal, every school lunch sandwich, every piece of toast tasted like bug repellent. Was it my imagination? Maybe. But as far as I was concerned, from then on food from our kitchen was contaminated.

Ninth grade was a blur. Having achieved freshman status I should have been thrilled to be in high school. But nothing thrilled me. I went from home to school and back home in a robotic manner. One afternoon I actually got lost and started to panic. I also was incensed. Why in the hell did we have to be here? Back home I knew where the high school was and would never have had this problem. I scowled and muttered my fury as I went up one street and down the other.

Somehow, I found my way and arrived at our apartment. Panic dissolved into frustration. I kicked off my shoes and threw my books on the table. My mother and sister hadn't gotten home yet and I was completely alone.

Tawk the Tawk

As a New Yorker, and one from Long Island, I had an accent that other kids found unintelligible. I also sported a chip on my shoulder a mile wide. I came from a metropolitan area that was home to people from all over the world. Here, there were only white kids or kids with Indian blood. Early marriage was the norm and college was a very distant dream. Many kids owned horses and rode all over unmarked land, but, I told myself smugly, they would be completely lost in the subway.

At the time, New York was going through racial unrest, which informed my mother's political outlook, and therefore mine. Many of my positions were incomprehensible to my classmates, as made obvious during a required speech I delivered in sociology class. As I spoke on riots and the attacks that police and firemen were experiencing, I saw frowns appear and heard mutterings. My fellow students viewed me as a racist. They believed I exaggerated and embellished the condition. Our worlds clashed and it was a foregone conclusion that I would be the loser in this ideological battle.

I only made one friend while in Colorado. Her name was Karen—not to be confused with St. Joseph's Karen—and she was as much of an outcast as was I. Colorado Karen was chunky and wore thick glasses and had the "look" that destined her to be unpopular. She was pale with flat blonde hair that lay thinly on her scalp. We were drawn together by our mutual need to feel accepted by *somebody*; other than that we had nothing in common. But we spent time at each other's homes and found things to talk about, as is the universal experience of teenage girls.

One Friday afternoon I walked home with Karen for a sleepover. On our way we passed graffiti on the sidewalk; someone had written in blue chalk "SUCK." I thought that was ridiculous and said so. "Why did someone write that?" It seemed so random. You might as well write "noodle" or some other word unrelated to anything else. Karen then proceeded to tell me the sexual connotation of the word.

I was floored. The mental image it evoked didn't even make sense to me. What were the mechanics of such an act? I told her she was wrong, that people didn't really *do* that. Karen assured me that yes, people do, and probably my parents did too. We walked in silence the next few blocks as I digested this new information with equal parts revulsion and intrigue.

When got to her house we went straight to her room, slumped on the floor, and chatted. Eventually her mother called us to supper and we sat at the table with her parents and younger brother. We had a nice meal, although the father was quiet and busied himself solely with eating. There was some small talk but it seemed stilted. This was very different from meals at my home, during which there was much animated conversation.

After supper Karen and I went back to her room. Suddenly the door banged open and her mother was in the doorway, swaying slightly, a cocktail glass in hand. "What are you girls talking about?" she demanded. "I bet Karen is telling you that her mother is a drunk. Well, I'm not," she slurred. "I just like a little drink with my dinner."

I felt as stunned as if I had been slapped across the face. I saw bright red spots pop up on Karen's cheeks and quickly looked away. Her mother, eyes watery and step unsure, turned unsteadily around, bumped into the wall, and closed the door.

Mortified for Karen, I wished I was home. My mother rarely indulged in hard liquor. I had never seen anyone drunk before. The rest of the evening passed uneventfully and I never told my mother what had happened. But from there on out, Karen and I got together at my house.

Tripping the Light Fantastic

I said that my mother rarely indulged in hard liquor but she did imbibe of the grape. She was so frugal in her intake that we never had more than one bottle of wine in the house at a time. Of course, her "stock" needed replacing now and then. Therefore, one afternoon on her way home from her teaching job, she stopped at the liquor store to buy a new bottle. Purchase in hand (in the obligatory brown paper bag) she emerged from the establishment.

Now this store happened to be on a busy street. The same street, as a matter of fact, as the school in which she taught. Gripping the bag, my mother crossed a concrete island to get to the parking lot. Or intended to. As it happens, she missed the curb, stumbled, and then landed in a heap on the ground, holding on to the bag with all her might.

"Oh my God," as she told me later, "I hope none of my parents were driving by. I looked slightly soused." Apparently she dodged that bullet because neither her principal nor any board member ever made mention of it.

A Pernicious Plot

Colorado Karen and I were thrown together by circumstance, not because we sought each other out. We were two lost, ostracized loners that didn't fit in with any group of our peers. Whereas Karen was a depressed girl who mainly looked at her feet if people spoke to her, I exuded an aura of defiance and superiority. I was not some hayseed girl hot to get a ring on her finger.

Inwardly I seethed at the situation in which I found myself. I did not want to be in this school or even in this state, for that matter. I was angry and scared but determined to keep those emotions pushed down to the deepest part of my psyche, never to worm their way up to the surface.

Until they did, in one ugly, shameful episode.

There was a certain girl in both our classes that neither Karen nor I could stand. She was quiet, studious, and friendly if spoken to. She wasn't particularly "cute," the standard by which teenagers assign a level of acceptance, but her other qualities overrode her lack of physical attributes. She was utterly inoffensive and therefore Karen and I mutually targeted her as the object of our contempt.

As it happened, her locker was right next to mine. I hatched a plan. I told Karen I would watch the girl as she ran the combination to her lock, and therefore could gain access. Karen thought that was brilliant. And so I did. I surreptitiously eyed the device as she innocently turned the mechanism right, left, and right again. I got it! Now all we had to do was figure out what wicked act we were going to perpetrate.

I am ashamed to say that we came up with an idea that causes me to shrink inside myself when I think of it, even today. One afternoon, as all the kids were getting to their next class, I pretended to be looking for something in my locker. As soon as the hallway emptied out I spun the combination to the girl's locker and quickly messed up the inside. Papers were ripped, books were upended and her jacket turned inside out. I couldn't wait for her to click the door open and discover our little surprise. At the end of the day I hung around waiting for our moment of triumph.

She came to her locker, and worked to open it, completely unaware of what was waiting for her. She opened the door and started to reach inside.

Her hand froze and her mouth twitched ever so slightly. There was no scream. She didn't drop her books, nor did she start to cry. She slammed the door shut, turned sharply, and went down a hallway. I moved away from my locker but stayed within sight to see what happened next.

She reappeared with a teacher and soundlessly reopened her locker to display the evil deed I had done. The exultant victory I had anticipated never materialized. I felt nothing but shame. There was no swelling of pride nor sense of vindication. The dawning realization that this was not who I truly was made me physically sick. I had tried to make this innocent girl feel as victimized as I was but the only thing I had accomplished was to reveal my own inadequacy and self-hatred. I waited for the inevitable punishment. Certainly, as the closest neighbor to her locker I was suspect. But it never came.

I wished it had.

...to Soothe the Savage Breast

One good memory of my time in the West is going to the library in Colorado Springs. The library had a collection of records of many different genres. You could check them out or listen to them right there, in a pleasant area furnished with upholstered chairs. A set of headphones was available and one could sit in plush comfort, put a record on the turntable, and enjoy the music. One specifically sticks in my mind, the opera *The Bartered Bride* by Smetana.

Headphones in place, legs tucked up under me, I listened in musical solitude to the bright notes of the overture and the dulcet tones of the singers. I followed along with the libretto and dreamily floated away on a euphoric cloud. In that moment I didn't worry about not having friends, or missing New York, or pudgy misfits with alcoholic mothers, or roach spray in the kitchen.

Minks, Appliances, and Fireworks

In order to supplement her teaching salary, my mother took a part-time job in the local Sears & Roebuck. There was a need in the fur department, so that's where she started. However, the patrons with perfectly permed hair and loaded pocketbooks did not appreciate my mother's unpretentious and… earthy approach to *haut couture*. Remember, this was the woman who wore men's eyeglasses and eschewed any form of makeup.

She was quickly relocated to the large appliances department.

As a result, my sister and I were left on our own many nights, and some weekends. But we felt safe in our little apartment and managed to entertain ourselves. I perfectly recall the New Year's Eve my mother was working at a babysitting job. It was inky black out and the countdown quickly approached.

With about 20 seconds 'til midnight our phone rang. It was Mommy. She told us to go to our bedroom and look out the window. As we did, suddenly the summit of Pike's Peak lit up with a majestic display of fireworks. It was magical. We squinted through the darkness, the pinnacle of the mountain erupting red, green, yellow, blue.

"I love you, girls," my mother said. "Happy New Year."

This rare display of affection took me by surprise. My heart soared with the rockets and fire fountains and missiles.

You Can

Go Home

Again

Upping Sticks

Not long after New Year's Eve, my mother got a phone call from Mom back in New York. My grandfather had suffered a stroke that paralyzed the right side of his body. He also had lost his ability to speak. My grandmother was not coping well and although my uncle Ronny lived in the house he was no help or comfort to her. Mommy decided to return to New York and move in with my grandparents in the Bronx.

This turn of events caused me to feel conflicted. I was ecstatic to leave this God-forsaken place but I was upset about my grandfather. Sadly, any euphoria I felt about returning to civilization was short-lived.

After hanging up from one of the conversations with my grandmother, Mommy informed us that she had secured a teaching job in upstate New York, in Ossining. Paula would commute north with her to attend the middle school, and I was to be enrolled in the Catholic school on Pelham Parkway.

I could barely process this information. I burst into tears, ran into our room, and threw myself on the bed. I couldn't believe it. All the nightmares I had about St. Joseph's Academy rushed over me and I was crushed under the weight of those memories. Any elation I had felt about returning to New York evaporated. But there was nothing I could do about it. At age 13 I was powerless over my own life and subject to the whims and wiles of every adult who came into it.

The day of the Great Return arrived and in late December my mother once again loaded up our clothes, a few essentials, and our recently acquired cat. Off we set in a Ford Cortina (the trusty and faithful Biscayne having finally given up the ghost). The morning was a western winter gray with the threat of snow in the air. My mother grimly pointed the car in the direction of the highway and our trip began. This must have been a tremendous blow to my mother. She had wanted to get out of New York, away from her parents, and have a new start in life.

She loved the wilderness and the mountains. She adored the deep blue of the sky. Colorado Springs, although an immature and underdeveloped city by New York standards, was a university town and did offer some urban amenities. She had taken us horseback riding and exploring. We often visited the Garden of the Gods, her particular favorite. We enjoyed free rein of the library at the University of Colorado. We fed winter-starving deer out of hand at the Royal Gorge Bridge.

Mommy loved every minute of our time in Colorado, even while hawking washers and dryers. But she understood — at least this time — her responsibility as a daughter, even to parents with whom she had a stormy, unhealthy relationship.

And so we made our way east, stopping at the occasional motel and even pulling off to the side of the road for quick naps. Getting ever closer to our destination, we crossed into Ohio. We drove for several hours and then as the thin blue of the winter sky gradually ceded to orange and pink with the setting sun, my mother determined it was time to stop for the evening. We pulled off the highway in a town named Zanesville, which made us giggle.

As we drove in search of lodging, our silliness turned somber. It was a weird place. It had the look of an Alfred Hitchcock set. We could imagine swarms of birds attacking our car, or a deranged innkeeper showing us to our room. My mother's opinion was that this was the kind of place where we could get murdered in our beds and she determined that we would not be spending the night in this town. (My apologies to what I am sure are the fine people of Zanesville. I'm certain our impressions were only brought on by over-active imaginations that could be blamed on road fatigue.) We returned to the highway and continued on toward the Pennsylvania border, where we found refuge in a town that my mother deemed more safe and hospitable.

A Bittersweet Reunion

Pennsylvania seemed interminable. No matter how much time passed we never seemed to get closer to the eastern border! I could not wait to see my grandmother. I suggested that we show up and surprise her but my mother said that would be too great a shock. Instead, when we were close Mommy pulled into a gas station and called to announce our imminent arrival.

Finally we made it! We pulled up to the house on Harding Avenue and stiffly eased ourselves out of the car, Paula clutching the cat. I ran to the door and rang the bell. My grandmother opened it, saw us, and instantly burst into tears. To my utter surprise, she and my mother fell into each other's arms. We made our way inside after maneuvering suitcases, pillows, and empty food containers from the car. My uncle Ronny, as usual, was lying on the living room carpet, watching TV. He looked up and said hello but made no move to greet us with a hug or offer of help. I didn't care—I was just glad to be out of the car and out of Colorado.

Things were not the same at 2925 Harding Avenue. Mom looked thin and frail. The dining room was now Morris' bedroom, complete with hospital bed, wheelchair, and portable toilet chair. He was perpetually dressed in pajamas and bathrobe, and spent his days either on the bed or hunched over in the wheelchair. His right hand was strapped to a plastic form meant to prevent his fingers from curling into a fist. Mom was relieved to relinquish the chores of shaving Morris and combing his hair to my mother, who took care of these and his other ablutions before her commute to work. Morris intermittently was either at home or back at the hospital, as his medical condition dictated. When he was home, I determinedly avoided looking at him.

Settling In

After a few days of unwinding and unpacking, Mommy got down to business. She enrolled Paula in Anne M. Dorner Middle School, which was conveniently located across the lot from my mother's new place of employment, Claremont Elementary. I was registered at my new Catholic school, Mother Butler.

New York City doesn't have school buses, so students are issued passes for the public transit system. I had to take two different buses to get from our house to the school; a transfer at Westchester Square was involved. The first day of school Mom and I crossed the street to the bus stop opposite our house. She rode with me to ensure my safe arrival and to show me how to make the transfer.

Whereas St. Joseph's was a bucolic estate populated by habit-clothed nuns, Mother Butler was right on Pelham Parkway, directly across from Jacobi Hospital, where my grandfather was a patient. It was all concrete and wire fencing. Cars whizzed by and planes flew overhead.

We made our way to the principal's office where I became an official student. Not a habit was to be seen; all the staff wore street garb, blending nun and layperson. After the paperwork I was told I would be assigned a "buddy" to help me get acclimated. A call was made to a classroom and I met Virginia for the first time. She had olive skin, long dark brunette hair, and a heart-shaped face. What impressed me most, however, was the black eyeliner encircling her almond eyes. This would never have been allowed at St. Joseph's — my first inkling that perhaps Mother Butler might negate the tortures I underwent in that Brentwood prison.

Virginia was animated and very friendly, allaying anxiety about this new school. My shoulders relaxed and my breathing suddenly returned to normal. I hadn't realized how my body had tensed in response to the dread I felt. We went up a flight of stairs and into what was my first class at Mother Butler.

Mother Butler was the best school experience of my life. All the girls were so friendly. And there was no communication problem — their "accents" were music to my ears. I can't recall if any of my teachers were nuns. My favorite was Miss Perotta, who taught English. She was young and animated and enthusiastic and I loved every minute of her class.

Our science teacher was male (so obviously, not a nun!) and whoever he is, I hope he received a medal at his retirement. We tortured that poor man. One incident sticks out in my mind as particularly sinister. He was summoned to the office to take a call from his wife. One of my classmates was in the office at the same time and managed to hit the intercom button. The entire school was treated to their conversation. When he returned he was beet red from the neck up, including his ears. Oh, we had such a laugh over that.

Another time one of the girls hid in the classroom closet, and jumped out right in front of him. I swear, he almost had a coronary on the spot. He either had an incredible reserve of fortitude, or needed that job badly because otherwise I don't know how he endured all our shenanigans.

In the spring we were invited to a retreat in upstate New York. We were bused up to a convent, a lovely place ideal for prayer and reflection, where we were to spend a weekend.

It was a wonderful getaway.

But...

We did not pray, nor did we reflect.

And we were invited never to return.

Jukebox, Smokes, and Taps

There was a deli close to the school, and almost every morning as I disembarked from the bus I made my way there. It was mobbed with Mother Butler students, all in uniform, lining up for breakfast. Most of us ordered the same thing—a buttered hard roll and a cup of coffee.

Lunch time was awesome. We ate in the basement and were served cafeteria style. The order of operation was to grab a tray, lay it on the metal rack, and make our way around the counter, indicating to the (longsuffering) cafeteria ladies what we wanted. The little paper cups of macaroni salad were a particular favorite of mine. The best thing, though, was the jukebox. There was actually a working jukebox—no coins required—stacked with all the latest records: "My Cherie Amour" by Stevie Wonder; "Ain't No Mountain High Enough" by Marvin Gaye and Tammy Terrell; "Love Child" by the Supremes; "Cloud Nine" by the Temptations... We'd eat our lunch and then get up and dance to the music.

Mother Butler is also where I learned the "right" way to smoke. I don't remember where I got cigarettes from—did I steal any from Mom? Did I buy them at the deli? In any event, I had cigarettes. So I lit up and pulled on the filter. The first time the girls saw me do this they laughed. What was so funny? Turns out I hadn't mastered the art of the inhale. So they showed me how to take the smoke in my lungs, and even demonstrated the finer points of an exquisite exhale by releasing the smoke through their noses and blowing smoke rings.

Determined to be as cool as the gang I immediately sucked that smoke in—and decidedly uncool—promptly had a coughing fit. They were very encouraging, however, assuring me that everyone does that at first, but then you get used to it. Ah, where would we be without true friends to light the way?

After the misery in Colorado, and despite the distress at home, I felt happy. I had found my niche. Thus, in the mornings I put on my uniform, singing along with Smokey Robinson or whoever was on the radio, did my hair, and carefully applied black eyeliner just like Virginia. Lastly, I buckled on my shoes.

Now, one of the unspoken but universally understood rules of dress at Mother Butler was the application of taps on our shoes. The louder the better. I had the cutest pair of brown strappy leather Mary Janes with a stamped pattern on the toe. (Forget the clodhoppers we were subjected to at St. Joseph's!) And on the heel? I had the shoemaker nail on the biggest pair of taps I could find. It took a special talent to master the specific step required to produce the perfect pinging of the tap, which I did. There was also the technique of dragging the heel in order to achieve the ideal metallic scratch, which added an extra element of cool.

So despite my grandfather's illness, my grandmother's depression, and my mother's exhaustion, I blissfully smoked and tapped my way through the last half of my freshman year.

I also blissfully fell in love.

The Hospital and First Love

Sick, with Dread

During one of Morris' stints at the hospital my mother determined it was appropriate for me to visit, but not Paula; she felt my sister was too young. Morris was in Jacobi Hospital which, as I said earlier, was right across Pelham Parkway from Mother Butler. The day rolled around when I was to go to the hospital and to prepare me, my mother told me that I might not be able to recognize Morris because he had changed so dramatically.

That chilly afternoon we approached the front door of the hospital. The building loomed like a brick and glass monster, the embodiment of my fears in seeing Morris in… what state? I imagined the electronic doors were jaws ready to swallow unwitting victims. As my mother, grandmother, and I entered the lobby I smelled, rather than saw, the hospital.

The odor of mingled antiseptic, boiled food, sickness, cigarette smoke, floor cleaner, and anxious hope was like the suffocating caress of an imperious lover. My other senses were crushed. I fought to emerge from under its oppressive weight, and gradually my eyes focused on the scene in the lobby.

Sunshine poured through the plate windows, but it held no warmth. Rows of molded plastic chairs tinted in artificially cheerful hues were bolted to the floor. Their salmon and avocado tones reeked of despair and forced congeniality. Visitors sat in lines and craned their necks to make stilted conversation, like cackling birds clinging to phone wires. Even though I was 14 I unconsciously moved closer to my mother.

We made our way to the elevator, and I uneasily anticipated the final leg of our journey.

To make sure I understood what lay ahead, my mother reiterated, "You won't recognize your grandfather." The perpetual lines between her eyes deepened. "He's not the person you remember," she intoned hollowly. She shifted the paper bag she was carrying to her other hand; it contained a jar of my grandmother's homemade soup.

As the elevator ascended I tried to collect my thoughts. *Should I smile at him?* I wondered. *No... he might think I'm heartless. Should I look concerned? No... he might think I'm upset. Will he even notice whether or not I'm smiling? Will he recognize me?* My hands became clammy, and in that metal box I felt ensnared like a trapped animal.

On a Rollercoaster

The slow ascension to the fifth floor was not unlike the deliberate, steady rise to the top of an amusement park ride. Instead of the exultant release of the downward plunge, however, there was an anticlimactic jerk as the car reached its destination. A cheerless, discordant ding announced our arrival and the dull monotone of sliding steel left a gaping wound for us to walk through. I stepped out like a prisoner preparing to hear her sentence, my mother and grandmother standing sentry on either side of me.

A tornado of impressions attacked my senses. What I had inhaled in the lobby was but a counterfeit of the malodorousness I encountered now; the dead and dying have a smell all their own. A sick pea-green color pervaded the walls, the linoleum, the curtains on the windows, and the drapes separating beds. In contrast to the efficient bustling of the nurses, patients lined the hallway with resigned—in some cases unconscious—patience.

In an effort to preserve a modicum of dignity, the patients were segregated by sex, so all the faces I encountered in this wing were male. I was gripped by a building panic as I searched one face and then another. My mother was right; I would not recognize my grandfather! He could not be found here! These men were so old... they had rubber bones, it seemed, since they could not sit erect in their wheelchairs. Their eyes were mostly vacant, and held no memories.

I saw one man who appeared to be the same height as Morris. I turned timidly to my mother.

"Is that him?" I whispered. I spoke in the same hushed and reverent tones I used in church.

"Of course not," my mother chided.

The walk down the hallway seemed interminable. At the very last room, on the left, my mother guided me to the door. As through a tunnel, I saw a wheelchair facing the window. The man in it made no effort to acknowledge our presence. His gray head lolled oddly to one side.

"Hello, dear," my grandmother offered timorously. She spoke as if this man were a stranger, and not her husband of 30-odd years. She bent over the chair and tentatively kissed his cheek.

"Look who's here to visit you," my mother chirped, as if I had asked to come along.

I hung back, heart pounding, unwilling to confront my grandfather's face. "Come say hello to your grandfather," my mother cheerfully insisted.

No! I screamed inside myself. Outwardly, I copied the plastic smile I now saw on both my mother's and grandmother's faces. I took a step closer.

Almost in slow motion, the man who used to be my grandfather looked up at me with milky eyes. He hadn't been shaved that morning, and gray-white stubble poked through his lower face like miniature needles trying to escape his skin. He wore pajamas and slippers, the uniform of the prisoner-sick. The fingers of his right hand curved obediently around a plastic board, and the hand lay uselessly in his lap. My fear and revulsion dissolved and a torrent of pity swept through me.

My grandfather met my gaze and I could see vague confusion and shame in his eyes. I bent over to kiss him and recognized the feel of his grizzled cheek. Yes, this was the same man who used to slip me money for ice cream.

Why, I know him, I realized in slight surprise. *He's in a wheelchair, but he looks the same.* Somehow, I thought he would have had a different face.

"Look what I've brought," my grandmother offered. She continued to prattle nervously while tucking a paper napkin under her husband's chin. She uncapped the jar of soup and for a brief moment, the smell of familiarity filled my nostrils.

The aroma—delicious beefy broth with chunks of meat, ditalini, and tomatoes—seemed incongruous in this pea-green, sterile sick room. This scent belonged in our kitchen, with the rest of the family crowded around the table, grating cheese and buttering Italian bread.

But I watched in detached fascination as Mom fed her husband. His tongue flattened and barely thrust forward as the spoon neared his mouth. A little rivulet of broth trickled down his stubbled chin and stained the paper bib.

I sat gingerly on the end of the hospital bed and waited for the feeding to be over. As I sat there, forgotten, watching this new family ritual, my essence folded in upon itself, like being swallowed by a black hole. Gripped by a new panic, I imagined I would helplessly implode if left in this room much longer.

Mercifully, the feeding was cut short when Morris waved away the soup spoon. After his chin was wiped clean and the bib removed, my mother moved in like a relief pitcher. She brandished an electric razor, and while she performed her duty Mom sank into a corner chair.

Through all this activity Morris sat passively, as if this were being done to someone else and he was merely a member of the audience, staring out the window like it was a stage. In an effort to pull Morris back to the present, my mother decided it was time to engage him in conversation. She asked him pointed questions and he laboriously attempted to answer.

He opened his mouth, and to my horror nothing came out but a high, thin, whiny babble. Incredulously, my mother responded as if what he had "said" was coherent. This was too much. I felt as if I were living inside a Dali painting; everything was real but distorted.

"Wouldn't you like to take Morris for a walk?" my mother asked me.

It was a question, but I knew I was obligated to obey. "A change of scene will do you good," she continued. Was she talking to me or him? Morris whined a response in his new voice as I carefully wheeled his chair around and headed out the door. I retraced my earlier route to the elevator since there really was nowhere else to go. The other old men guarded their posts along the halls. Mental exhaustion and mindless pacing with the chair numbed me into a trance-like state.

Thunderstruck

Suddenly, my eye was jolted by a shock of jet black hair set among the rows of gray. My pace quickened as I sought to look at this young man. Emboldened I gazed directly into a smooth brown face and was surprised to find a pair of ebony eyes staring back. I reddened when he winked at me. I walked past quickly and he, in turn, wheeled himself around with the deftness of an acrobat. He remained a short distance behind and kept up a steady stream of questioning interspersed with appreciative whistles and soft kissy noises.

"Hey, baby, what's your name? Ooh, you got nice legs. Where you goin', baby?" He chattered on in a patois of Spanish and English.

I kept my head down and pretended a complete fascination with the floor tiles. When I arrived at Morris' room my heart was pounding and I was oddly out of breath. The young man pulled right up to the doorway, took a long impudent look into the room, and then smoothly wheeled away. My mother was immediately on the attack.

"Who was that? Why was he down here? Ignore him — he looks like nothing but trouble." Her case was presented, tried and decided. Just like that.

On the ride home the passing scenery was a blur. My grandfather's condition, the repugnance of the hospital, Mom's sorrow, were all forgotten. I looked out the car window and saw those two ebony eyes staring back at me. The wheels of the bus driving in the next lane transformed into the spoked gray wheels of a finely maneuvered chair.

After a few more trips I came to a decision.

"I think I could visit Morris by myself tomorrow," I offered tentatively. "I can walk over from school and catch a later bus home. That could give you two a break."

My mother was silent a moment, mentally recalculating the logistics of the day. I held my breath, waiting.

"That might be nice," she conceded. "But I'd like you to be home before dark."

Getting to Know You

The next visit to the hospital I eagerly took my grandfather for a stroll up and down the hallway.

In the common area was a maze of old men and women with vacant stares. Cigarette smoke swirled around the hallway. My step was bold as I searched among the clouded eyes for a pair of black alert ones.

Eventually, a smooth brown face emerged and all my confidence melted into caution. What was I playing at? This was not like me! I feigned interest in the top of my grandfather's head. My heart was pounding and my breathing became shallow. I escorted my grandfather back to his room, the admirer following a short pace behind. When I got into the room I saw "him" give one last look — a brazen one, I thought — and then he was gone.

The next afternoon I walked to the hospital from school. Spring was beginning to bud, but in spite of the slight chill I found myself warm and flushed as a June day. The front doors slid open invitingly at my approach. Sunlight streamed through the windows and diffused everything with a cheerful yellow glow. With purposeful intent I strode to the elevators and eagerly stepped into the first available car. The ride to the fifth floor was smooth, and during the ascent I evened out the pleats in my uniform skirt and tugged the vest down over my waist. The elevator came to a gentle stop, and I stepped out without hesitation.

I started down the hall toward my grandfather's room, my eyes searching the hall attentively. Nothing had changed — gray heads and clouded eyes lined the hallway. Cigarette smoke hung in the air. Nurses fussed, like uniformed mother hens, and the PA system squawked a gibberish of codes and announcements.

But I was different. A head of black hair and a pair of intense almond eyes exhilarated me and quickened my step.

"Hey baby, you come back for another visit? Who's that ol' man? Why don' you come and visit *me*?"

I turned around and there he was, rolling his chair back and forth like it was a street rod straining at a red light. I allowed myself my first close look at him. He was not much older than I was. Shiny, jet black hair framed his round face. Thick curly lashes fringed sparkling eyes. His mouth was full and a deep red more expected on a girl. He wore a white tee shirt that accented muscular arms, and tan pants that covered legs I later learned had been crushed in a train accident.

"C'mon baby, sit with me a minute. Look, there's no one over here."

We stopped by an alcove that served as a waiting area outside a little chapel. I followed him to a short row of chairs and nervously sat down. He positioned his chair directly in front of me.

"What's your name?" he asked, softly.

I half-whispered my reply, and when he repeated it back to me it trilled like a song. He said his name was Nelson.

"Who you visit here?" he inquired.

"My grandfather. He had a stroke."

And so we went back and forth: advancing, pulling back, becoming bolder. Only when supper trays were brought around did time intrude. My mother's warning about the dark jolted me back to reality.

"I have to leave now," I told him, thinking incongruously of Cinderella and the stroke of midnight.

"Come back tomorrow, okay baby? Okay?"

"I'll try," I promised.

Falling Deeper and Deeper...

And so I did. Almost every day, after school, I walked across Pelham Parkway to the hospital. To assuage any guilt I felt for duping my mother I would occasionally visit my grandfather, but most times I sat with Nelson in the quiet corner by the chapel. We would hear each other's confession and offer penitential prayers of promise. We practiced the sacrament of love with venial and then venerable kisses. The incense of his skin filled my nostrils and I felt consumed by his spirit.

As the weather warmed we spent time outside. It was a vibrant spring—flowers were imbued with earthy shades of purple and red. Deep green grass carpeted the lawns. A brilliant gold sun haloed each of our heads. The days gradually lengthened, which meant each afternoon I could stay a little longer.

On one of my visits to Nelson he said he had something to ask me.

"I wan' you to meet my mother," he said shyly.

Oh, that's nice, I thought.

"Sure," I smiled. Who could resist those soulful brown eyes?

On my next planned visit, there she was, sitting with her son. She was short and older than I would have thought. She had the same deep brown eyes, but ones tinged with worry. She didn't speak a word of English, so smiling and gesturing became our mode of communication.

I never thought to question it, but I wonder why Nelson wanted us to meet. Did he think we had a future? I believe he was as much in love with me as I was with him. Did he want to please his mother, showing her that he had a "nice" girlfriend? It makes me sad to ponder and I think of Nelson from time to time, with the bittersweet pang of lost teenage love.

...And Hitting Bottom

On those days when I went to the hospital with my mother and grandmother, I would pretend not to know Nelson. The two women would have only seen a Puerto Rican idol and condemn the young love as a false religion. So I would walk past him, eyes fixed on the floor, my heart feeling like stone. He was bolder though, and sometimes would daringly follow us down the hall. This irritated my mother, who would frown and stare daggers at him.

"I don't know what that PR thinks he's doing, but you stay away from him," my mother ordered.

In the innocence of youth, and with intense confidence, we two young lovers had faith that we would find absolution. I was therefore totally unprepared for Armageddon.

The afternoon of reckoning the clouds thickened and became black. Rain poured down. The thunder was so deep it rattled the heart inside my chest. Nelson and I were forced indoors where we sat together, holding hands, by a row of chairs in a hall opposite the elevator doors. It was a day for quiet conversation and basking in each other's company. A boy with mangled legs and a girl with a mangled life. Occasionally the elevator doors would open and shut, discharging passengers. Content in our rosy haze of love, I saw the doors slide open again, and my eye became unwillingly fixed on a familiar figure marching purposefully in our direction.

My back stiffened involuntarily and I sat upright as the face came into focus. I dropped Nelson's hand and rose to my feet. My mother came to an abrupt halt directly in front of us. Her face mimicked the storm raging outside.

"I came to visit Morris..." I stammered lamely. A dozen excuses shuffled through my mind, and I picked the one that flashed across my mind's eye. "...he was sleeping so I came out here to sit..."

My mother's face killed the rest of my words. "Come with me," she demanded through clenched teeth. She wheeled around and marched back up the corridor as decisively as she had made her approach. Like a lamb to the slaughter, I submissively followed.

I turned once and saw Nelson as through reversed binoculars. As he faded away I gave him a small, limp wave. From the distance I could not tell if he had waved too, or even seen me. My heart fell as we descended the elevator in silence. I fought to hold back the bile forcing its way up my throat.

When we stepped out into the lobby, I could smell the steam of bland food coming from the hospital kitchen. The empty plastic chairs looked forlorn, abandoned. No sunlight came through the streaked plate windows. Cigarette smoke stung my eyes and burned my nostrils. As I passed through the electronic doors into the grayness of the afternoon, I noticed a patch of pink tulips had been ripped up from their flower bed and stepped on.

I could not understand why that made me cry.

Comes the Reaper

The human body can only endure so much, and inevitably, after years of smoking, hard work, and the recent strokes and heart attacks, my grandfather succumbed to the accumulated trauma. He died in April of 1969. Oddly enough, I don't have any particular emotion from his passing. Maybe it was a relief that the hospital bed would be out of the dining room. Or that the urinal bottle would be thrown away. Or perhaps because the schedule hanging in the kitchen to denote the time and amount of each medication was taken down.

Numb from Morris' death and the loss of Nelson, the following days passed in a haze. The Sisto Funeral Home made the requisite arrangements. There was the wake, a service, interment in Kensico Cemetery, the reception back at the house, then… what?

Each of us had to find a way to return to a life that wasn't overshadowed by the smell of antiseptics and the rattling of pill bottles. My mother resumed her commute to Ossining and I returned to Mother Butler. My grandmother roamed the house in a ghostly trance. May was mostly a blur, and then June arrived. School ended, and unbeknownst to me, life in the Bronx was also coming to a close.

Ossining

Bye-bye, Bronx

My mother hated living in the city, and understandably, she detested the daily commute. She therefore made it her mission to find a house in Ossining, where her school was located. Mom had lived her whole life in the City and spent many years in the Bronx in the first house she had ever owned, and did not want to leave. But she was so wrung out emotionally and physically that she didn't have the fortitude to put up a fight. Per usual, my mother won and found a house on a hilly street, Prospect Avenue. It actually was lovely, with pine trees on each side of the front entrance, a *very* precarious driveway, a deeply sloping backyard, and a deck to offer a gorgeous view of the Hudson River.

Mom hated it.

I hated it.

But no matter, Mommy loved it so that's where we were going to live. Mom's house was sold and the proceeds went to a down payment on #18. My grandmother's belongings—those my mother deemed fit to bring with us—were packed. We retrieved our possessions from storage. The move was not a once and done affair, however, as things migrated north—as my mother used to say—in dribs and drabs. Because of the erratic schedule, Paula and I found ourselves sleeping in the new house alone one night, on a pull-out couch.

We were petrified.

The silence was eerie. No drag-racing muscle cars. No overhead airplanes. No sirens. Just... crickets. The damn crickets!

I couldn't fall asleep. Every little creak the house made caused hair on the back of my neck to stand up.

A car door slammed; was it the pervert I was convinced was coming to get us? The eerie hoot of an owl caused me to jump.

In time, I did fall asleep but it was a fitful night spent on that couch.

Eventually the move was complete. My mother filled the house with things. *Her* books, *her* records, *her* furniture, *her* dishes. My grandmother's piano hadn't made the cut, nor had much of her belongings. Her own bedroom simply contained the suite from the Bronx, and an oil painting she had bought in France. No Italian dolls. No war medals. Just her bedroom suite, clothing, and sewing machine.

Our New Digs

Since there were just three bedrooms, Paula and I shared one as well as the double closet. A door, perpetually shut, separated my mother's room from ours. A short hallway led to Mom's room. We had two windows; one looked out onto the street and a large leafy tree filled the other. We arranged our beds side by side, separated only by a few inches. My mother's room, which also wasn't very big, had a queen-sized bed and a dresser bought in Colorado.

I loved spending time in my grandmother's room. Her four-poster bed was adorned with carved pinecones. The double dresser with a mirror stood along one wall and my grandfather's armoire, another. A lacy runner, feminine knickknacks, and the ubiquitous pack of Kent cigarettes graced the polished top of the dresser. Her sewing machine sat in front of a window and was next to her tiny walk-in closet. The mingled scent of perfume, bath powder, and unlit tobacco wafted around the room. We spent many an afternoon lying on the bed together, each engrossed in our own book, intermittently sharing our favorite passages.

The one bathroom was on the same floor as our bedrooms, which was convenient.

Both the basement and attic were unfinished, but more about that later.

On the first floor, the small enclosed entryway housed a coat closet. During the summer Mom placed mothballs in that closet; I hated the smell. Upon entering the house proper, one could turn left to the living room or right to a dining room. A small space adjoining the living room accommodated an organ my mother purchased. (Mom's piano would have fit nicely in there.) These two rooms had windows all the way around, which made them sunny and cheerful. The living room also held the long bookcase my mother had had built in Colorado. A couch, console TV, and high-backed easy chair completed the ensemble.

The kitchen contained the usual appliances, but I truly fell in love with the sink for some reason. Maybe it reminded me of the one at 50 Carmine—it was shallow with bumpy countertops on each side for draining dishes. Made of porcelain, it added character to the room. There were two doors to the outside; one to a small landing and the steep back stairs and one to the porch, which I suspected was a big selling point for my mother.

Our home at 18 Prospect Avenue.

The porch was large—it held a picnic table and benches, a few occasional chairs, and a glider. Also, being city people, we had a clothesline that ran from a post of the porch to a giant tree. But the best part was the view of the Hudson River. Sunsets were different every evening and simply spectacular. And at night we could see lights twinkling along the Palisades on the opposite side of the river. Of course as a teenager I didn't really care about the landscape. But I can see it in my mind's eye now and I miss it deeply.

Getting Our Bearings

As we did on Long Island, we would hop in the car and go exploring, this time with my grandmother in tow. We rode north up the Hudson and explored all the little charming towns dotting the river. We drove over to Connecticut to find a lake or shoreline of the Long Island Sound to sit by. Driving into Manhattan to shop or dine or attend a performance of one kind or another was a snap. We toured West Point. We meandered around Bear Mountain. All worthy destinations, but upon my mother's announcing we were going for a trip I often rolled my eyes.

As we piled into the car I would feel disquietude. Would my mother and Mom get into a fight or would we all wind up laughing uproariously? One never knew on what road the emotional wind would blow us. There were times when something would set my mother off (did Mom ever goad her? I wonder…) and the screaming and crying and pounding on the steering wheel would commence. My mother would wipe away the tears that blurred her view and my grandmother would pull out her hankie from her purse. Paula would retreat into her own world and I… did what? Any emotional protective device I employed did its job; the memory has faded with the years.

Conversely, my mother or grandmother would comment on something. They both had a sharp sense of humor, although my mother's was overstated and Mom's understated. Again the tears would flow, but this time from laughter. Out would come Mom's handkerchief, and boy, could she blow that horn. Those were the lighthearted times. The uncertainty of which way things would wind up always had me on high alert.

My mother remained an avid gardener, determined to turn our yard into something beautiful. There was one stubborn shaded area, however, in which nothing would grow. Mommy determined groundcover was the answer.

Riding around, she spotted a hillside covered with pachysandra and decided that was the ticket. And look how much of it there was here! Why buy it when she could just dig some up and transplant it? It grew so fast it would replenish, and the plants would cover the bald patch in our yard.

Excitedly she described to Mom how they could go under the cover of darkness and nab some plants. At first Mom was hesitant but eventually won over by my mother's enthusiasm. So pails and gloves and spades — and flashlight — were gathered, and when night fell, off they went. Triumphantly they returned with enough pachysandra to solve the problem. Several days later my mother came home to tell Mom that she drove past the "scene of the crime," this time in daylight, only to discover that they had stolen plants out of the yard of a detective agency!

Ne suis pas une boulangère (I'm not a baker)

Along with gardening, my mother fancied herself an excellent cook and baker. I am here to remind you that she operated under grave misapprehension. She was a mediocre cook at best, but a terrible baker. In one instance, the aforementioned porch came in handy.

She had made a cake that was not only dry but as solid as stone. In other words, inedible. She decided that at least the birds and squirrels could peck and claw at it. She brought it to the railing of the porch and gave it a heave ho. Instead of falling apart as it hit the ground, however, the density of its mass caused it to bounce and roll down the slope. This is the stuff that family anecdotes are made of, passed down from one generation to the other.

A Sorry Soufflé

An equally outstanding unsuccessful attempt at dessert occurred when Mommy invited the secretary from her school over to watch home movies of our time in Colorado. Miss Smith lived with her elderly mother and sister. They were very prim women with a framed picture of Jesus on the wall — a blond, blue-eyed Jesus with a sappy expression, eyes looking woefully heavenward.

Mommy was determined to impress, so she decided — never having made one before — to make a soufflé. Did we have the requisite copper bowl in which to whip the egg whites? *No.* Did we have the confectioner's sugar to sweeten? *No.* Did Mommy know what she was doing? *No!* But those petty details never stopped the tour de force that was Mommy.

Miss Smith arrived and the soufflé was removed from the oven, whereupon we all watched it immediately sink in upon itself. Never let a minor detail like that impede!

"It will still taste good," my mother confidently assured us.

She put a dollop of homemade whipped cream on each portion and spooned out the not-a-soufflé and served the bowls. Now she understood why the recipe called for superfine sugar and not granulated sugar. The resulting coagulated mess was as sandy as if it had first been rolled on one of Long Island's famous beaches.

Undaunted, my mother started up the film projector and proceeded to regale Miss Smith with our adventures in The Great West. As we watched the blue skies and mountain vistas roll by, we pushed the dessert around in our bowls in an attempt to make it appear that we had eaten some of it. After Miss Smith left we scraped the soppy mess into the garbage while Mommy unconcernedly laughed the incident off.

Just Keep it to Ourselves

On my birthday we went out to a lovely German restaurant in Valhalla. We enjoyed a delectable meal and then ordered coffee; it was time for dessert! Would we savor the famous Black Forest cake? The flaky apple strudel? Some rich Bavarian cream? No such luck. Mommy had decided she would make my cake and bring it with us.

The waitress emerged from the kitchen, holding aloft the lopsided confection. She placed it on the table along with a big knife and dessert plates.

As my mother cut into the cake, bright green pudding oozed from between the layers. It looked like pus.

"Doesn't this look good?" my mother exulted. "I put a pistachio filling inside. It's going to be delicious!"

The waitress blanched.

Just then we heard the strains of "Happy Birthday" from another table.

"Another birthday celebration!" observed Mommy.

She turned to the waitress. "After I cut this last slice, bring the cake over to the other table, with our compliments," she said to the waitress.

To her credit, our server declined, indicating they had already ordered their desserts. I don't know if that was true or not, but what I can testify to is that the waitress had no intentions of inflicting a cake that looked like it had a massive infection on those poor, unsuspecting people.

My mother's ability to be blithely unaware of her social faux pas was, in a way, admirable. No second guessing herself or deconstructing what might have gone wrong and how to amend things to avoid a duplication in the future. Ignorance truly is bliss.

California 2

Flying Solo

My second trip to California was in an altogether different class. The year was 1970 and by this time Wendy had moved there. She and my mother agreed I could go visit. Wendy said she would send a ticket in the mail; however, it was going to be in my mother's name since immediate family was allowed to fly free in those days; the guest only had to pay the tax on the fare. For this flight, I would be flying alone.

One summer Saturday my mother and Paula left the house early to take a trip to Long Island to visit Alyce, our erstwhile camping partner. Therefore, when the mail arrived, I was home by myself. Guess what was delivered that portentous day? One open-ended ticket to California, meaning the ticket could be used any time. I flew into action.

I walked downtown to the bank and withdrew money from my savings account. Loaded down with my loot I walked back home, which was all uphill. I was so sweaty when I arrived at the house that I had to take a shower. But there was one critical task to complete first—I had to figure out how to get to the airport. *The Yellow Pages!* Thank goodness for the phone book.

I flipped through and found the phone number for a local airport limo service. Fortunately, there was a driver available and we settled on a pickup time. Mind you, I had no idea if there would even be a flight available once I got to JFK. I showered, packed a suitcase, threw my money into a purse along with a comb, mirror, and lipstick. *Hmm... am I missing anything?* Oh yes—a note, letting my mother know where I was.

"Mommy, my ticket came today and I've left for California. Love, Ellen."

Right on time, the limo arrived. The driver was a very nice man and we had a great conversation on the way, until...

"So, you're going to California today, huh? That's pretty exciting."

"Yeah, my aunt works for Pan Am and sent me a ticket."

"So she's meeting you at the airport, right?"

"No, she lives in California. That's what I'm doing, going to visit her."

"Wait, you're flying out there on your own?"

"Yes, but it's OK. I left my mother a note explaining everything so she won't wonder where I am when she gets home."

"Wait a minute. Your mother doesn't know what you're doing? How old are you, anyway?"

"I'm 15."

I almost got whiplash as he slammed on his brakes. Good thing we weren't on the highway yet.

"I'm taking you back home! I can't be responsible if anything happens to you!"

It took some fast talking but I managed to convince my driver that I would be OK. My mother knew I would be going, we had been waiting for the ticket to arrive, I was used to making my way around Manhattan so this was no big deal, etc., etc., etc. He relented but very reluctantly.

At last we reached our destination and my driver let me out at the Pan Am terminal and wished me luck. (I wonder if *he* ever wonders if I made it.) I threaded my way to the ticket counter where a uniformed man stood behind the desk.

"Ticket, please."

I handed him my ticket.

"May I see some identification?"

Uh oh. Next hurdle to jump over. The best attack, I decided, was to take the offensive position; it's the best defense, right?

"Why do you need to see my ID? Is there something wrong?" I shot in my best "adult" voice.

The attendant licked his lips and his eyes darted sideways for an instant. (Aah, he's already on the ropes.) "Well, I just need to verify that the name on the ticket matches your identification."

Hmm… this might get tricky if I don't play my cards right.

I channeled my inner Mommy. "Are you insinuating I have a stolen ticket? Do you think I don't know my own name? What is the problem? You know, I'm a minor and I'm here by myself! My grandmother is waiting for me in California, and if I don't show up she's going to be upset! And if I can't get on that flight, what am *I* going to do? I don't have a ride back home and if anything happens to me it will be your fault!" I allowed my voice to rise with each question, hopefully imparting a sense of impending danger and disaster.

My ploy worked! He waved his hand and said, "Fine. Just get to the boarding gate." Amazingly it was that easy.

The Best Laid Plans…

I made my way to the gate and eventually my section was called for boarding. Now a seasoned traveler, I relaxed in my seat as the crew readied for takeoff. About 30 minutes into the flight a stewardess leaned over and asked if my name was Ellen. Surprised, I answered that yes, it was.

Apparently (obviously!) it had not occurred to me to call my grandmother, who was staying at my aunt's apartment in California to let her know I was coming. My mother had arrived back home, found my note, and took matters in hand. She called my grandmother, who quickly informed her that not only was my aunt not home — she was out of the country working on a flight — but that she had no idea I was on my way. It also had not occurred to me that I would need transportation to get from LAX to my aunt's apartment. My plans had gotten me financed, packed, to JFK and on the plane, but I hadn't thought about what would happen once I disembarked.

I'm not sure how the airline was contacted, but somehow the pilot had been radioed and he relayed the message to the stewardess, who subsequently relayed the message to me that there would be a ride waiting for me at LAX. Who was the ride? Well, I didn't know, since my grandmother didn't drive.

Although she was normally no good in an emergency, I later found out that in a panic Mom phoned a friend of my aunt's who kindly agreed to drive to the airport and get me. I was glad to hear it, but in my blissful naiveté it never dawned on me that my mother, grandmother, the airlines, the crew, and my aunt's friend were all working behind the scenes to get me safely situated in my home away from home.

To Mom's credit, she never castigated me once we connected. Maybe she was just so relieved I was safe (and probably emotionally drained) that she gave me a kiss and introduced me to my aunt's friend. We made it to the apartment and the evening ended without any further fuss.

My aunt was going to be away for a few more days so it was Mom and me on our own. Since, as I mentioned, Mom didn't drive, we spent two quiet days reading, playing cards and Scrabble, and basically enjoying each other's company.

Alone Again, Unnaturally

The evening of the second day, the phone rang. Mom answered it, and I watched as she listened… her grip on the receiver tightened as her mouth started to tremble and tears spilled from her eyes. The conversation was brief, and pretty much one-sided.

When she replaced the receiver on the phone's cradle, she turned to look at me; her mouth was working but no words came out. Tears overflowed and she finally told me that her brother Julie (Julius) had died. He had dropped dead right in his driveway; resuscitation had been futile.

Mom had an exceptional love for this brother (there were three of them) so this was a particular blow. There was no question about it — she would be flying home as soon as possible.

Early the next morning Mom was on the phone with Pan Am and was able to secure a family emergency ticket for a flight leaving that afternoon. She packed hastily and got a ride to the airport. (Was it the same friend? A taxi? I don't remember.)

I had only met Julie a couple of times and liked him immensely. He was friendly and had a gentle way about him. I could easily understand how my grandmother loved him so. I hurt for her, but I also felt great trepidation about staying on my own in this unfamiliar apartment complex. My grandmother had given me as much advice as her flustered state would allow (don't open the door, make sure the chain is on, be careful who you talk to on the telephone) but it did nothing to assuage my anxiety.

Eventually, night fell and after watching enough TV to make me drowsy, I went to bed. The bedrooms were in the back of the apartment, farthest from the front door. I began to think… what if someone tried to come in, would I hear them? I decided to sleep on the living room couch, close to the phone. Surely I could dial for help before someone was able to knock the door down, especially with the chain on! I spent a restless, uneasy night.

As usually happens, when morning arrived and I was still in one piece (as was the door) I felt chagrinned and even embarrassed by my unfounded fears. The sun was out, I had a whole apartment to myself, and Wendy was due home that afternoon.

A Whole Lotta Shakin' Goin' On

The remainder of my trip was — thankfully — less worrisome apart from one minor incident…

I am a very sound sleeper. Nothing wakes me. So it was most unusual when, in the middle of the night, I was awakened by a shaking. Was Wendy trying to get me up? I looked through unfocused, groggy eyes but did not see anyone in the room. Had I had a vivid dream? No, not that I could remember. Wait… there it was again! The room was definitely rolling. I went into Wendy's bedroom and woke her up.

"What's going on?" I half-whispered. "Everything is shaking and rolling."

Equally groggy, Wendy opened one eye — slightly — and said, matter of factly, "It's only an earthquake." Completely unfazed. Well, she wasn't worried, and it was still dark out, so I figured, *OK, I guess I'll go back to bed.*

In the morning, we were able to assess the damage. The walls were intact, and no pictures had fallen, but when we went outside we discovered a huge crack in the foundation of the complex's pool and a good deal of water had sloshed out.

While riding on the highway that afternoon I saw an impressive chunk of concrete on the shoulder of the road. It had been rattled off by the previous night's earthquake. *California is beautiful,* I mused, *but not enough to ever entice me to live here.*

Up, Up, and Away

We took an excursion to the Santa Monica Pier. It was beautiful. The blue of the water mirrored the blue of the sky. Impressive yachts bobbed gently in the slapping swell of the marina's water. We wandered leisurely, admiring the different shops and enjoying the scents of the various restaurants stationed around the pier. One of the shacks close to the water advertised helicopter tours around the area.

"Let's go!" enthused Wendy, who of course had many hours of flying under her belt, not only in jumbo jets and smaller passenger planes, but also little two-seaters and even a glider. I, on the other hand, had only ever been in jets, which seemed substantial and safe. Not to be outdone, however, I readily agreed.

We paid for our tickets and clambered into the helicopter, which had a bubble-shaped cockpit, meaning passengers were afforded a 360-degree view while airborne. There was a bench seat where Wendy and I sat together. As we buckled ourselves in, the pilot turned the ignition (or whatever it's called in a helicopter) and I could hear the blades whirring and whining. Faster and faster they went, and suddenly we were elevated off the ground.

I gritted my teeth and clutched Wendy's hand. More like seized. I dug in my nails, and held on for dear life. I feigned interest as Wendy excitedly pointed out this and that site of interest. I silently congratulated myself for maintaining an outward semblance of composure... until Wendy, yelling over the noise of the machine, asked the pilot how high up we were.

"Shut up!" I screamed. "Don't talk! Don't answer her! I don't want to know!"

There was a momentary silence, except for the damnable, incessant noise of the helicopter, and then Wendy burst out laughing. The pilot didn't say anything; I think he was shocked. We flew the rest of the tour in (relative) silence. When we came to rest once again on terra firma it was as if my sense had been restored.

I was mortified by my extreme reaction, and totally irritated with myself that I hadn't been able to enjoy the experience. It was a gorgeous day, the views from the air really were incredible, and had I been able to relax I would have appreciated the gentle turns and dips into which the pilot guided his craft. But so much of my life had been infected with fear and intimidation that what should have been a new and exciting experience was instead terrifying.

Hadn't I been warned about staying off rollercoasters because you could fall out of them to your death? Wasn't I told to only go ice skating in a rink because on a lake I could fall through the ice and drown? Aren't all strangers—and even some neighbors—to be distrusted and avoided? These lessons, pounded into my psyche, informed how I approached life. And they were not easily ignored or overcome. In any event, the ride was a complete debacle and to this day I have never been in another helicopter.

We visited Solvang, a Danish community with architecture, gardens, shops, and food that reflected and paid homage to the Danish culture. We drove around Santa Barbara and on the Pacific Coast Highway.

We spent a day at Olvera Street, with Mexican architecture, shops, roving musicians, and restaurants. But by far the most memorable excursion was to a private party; we were invited by one of Wendy's friends, another flight attendant who hailed from Sweden.

Trying on hatwear on Olvera Street.

It's a Happenin' Scene, Man

We arrived at the host's house; we had been preceded by a crowd of people, all of whom looked like for-real hippies. We parked our car on the grass and walked to a gate in the fence. A girl was waiting there, armed with a stamp and an inkpad. She stamped our foreheads with a purple flower. Thus christened, we walked through the gate into the throng.

The atmosphere was redolent of weed and love was in the air. I swore I could actually hear love beads clacking. I wore shorts and had borrowed a tee shirt from Wendy that said "HAWAII." I felt totally out of place. Some guy weaved his way over to me and said, "Cool shirt. Have you ever been to Hawaii?" I said I hadn't. He peered at me with eyes that were bloodshot and not quite focused. "I didn't think so," he said, and stumbled off. I felt like a total imposter.

Wendy was off talking to her friend and I was on my own. Never comfortable in social situations, this was beyond anything I had ever experienced. I wandered from one cluster of people to another, trying to find a spot in which I could hang out and be part of what was going on. Nothing doing.

As I made my way around I came to the area where lunch was being barbecued. A large pit had been dug in the earth and a long tree branch extended from one end of the hole to the other. The air above the pit was wavy from heat waves undulating up from a nicely seasoned fire. Threaded onto the branch was the carcass of some animal (lamb? pork? beef?) that was intended as the main course.

I watched, incredulous, as a guy with long, curly blond hair removed his tee shirt and wound it around a mop handle. Next to him on the ground was a bucket. His shirt now secured, he dipped it into the bucket, sloshed it around, and then proceeded to slop the now fully sauced tee shirt up and down the animal being barbecued. I went and found Wendy. "You gotta see this," I told her. I led her over to the fire pit.

"That's it," she said. "We're leaving." We threaded our way in and out of the various vehicles parked haphazardly around the lawn and found ours. "Well, I wasn't going to eat any of *that*," Wendy determined, "but I am hungry." We drove around until we found a diner and went in.

It hadn't occurred to us that with purple stamps on our forehead and the residual halo of weed wafting faintly about us, we might, well, attract a certain amount of attention. But by this time we were so hungry we didn't care. We sat in a booth and were given menus. I was happy to order a cheeseburger and fries, but Wendy, ever conscious of her figure, opted for lighter fare.

The waitress came over, prepared to take our order. I recited mine, and then Wendy said, "I'll have the 'No Sandwich Sandwich' on rye."

The waitress stared at her with a "wry" expression. "That is served without bread, hon," she said. "Hence the name." I thought I detected a slight eye roll.

"Oh!" Wendy replied. Recovering her composure she said, "That will be fine." As if we were in a 3-star Michelin restaurant or something. When the waitress walked off we exploded with laughter.

When we got back to Wendy's apartment she said that we were not setting foot in her house with clothes that stank and might possibly have fleas hidden among the folds. She made me strip down right outside her door (she did as well) and we stepped over the threshold, naked as jaybirds. Thank heavens that hers was an end unit and hidden from sight. We showered and scrubbed our heads (to ward off any lice that might have caught a ride home with us) and then took our clothes right to the laundry room.

In between excursions we spent our time reading, playing Scrabble, cooking, and watching TV. All too soon, though, it was time for me to leave. I cherished the time I had had Wendy to myself. On the day of my departure, she drove me to the airport, we said our goodbyes, and I walked to the boarding gate, through the jetway, and settled into my seat on the plane.

The flight home afforded me time to reflect on my experience in California and the return to New York. A picture of myself as a kid playing in Wendy's room came to mind—the past couple of weeks had awakened that memory. This time, however, I was invited to play in that world openly. The glow I felt didn't come only from the California sun.

But as we flew into the grayness of the eastern sky it began to dissipate, as surely as the concrete skyline of Manhattan that came into view.

Ossining Redux

On the Sidelines

So these were my high school years. I hated them but a lot of my loneliness and isolation was self-imposed. Many, if not most, of my classmates had known each other since elementary school and had forged bonds. Many were also related, as Ossining was a small town. And as happens in high schools everywhere, cliques were formed. There were the cheerleaders, the athletes, the artists, the druggies, the brainiacs, the rebels... and those were the white kids.

There was a goodly black population as well: some had joined the Black Panthers, girls comprised the Pep Squad, guys on the football teams. It was as if there was an unwritten law that the X groups were for the white kids and the Y groups were for the black ones—except for football, the great equalizer.

So where did I fit in? Nowhere, really. I had a few friends that I hung around with but we didn't belong anywhere. I guess we were our own group. I did, however, have both black and white friends. To me, if we shared interests and could get along, that was all that mattered.

I wish I had joined some of the clubs. How would things be different if I had belonged to one? But I was too shy and too insecure and too, well, unpracticed in the art of making friends and being a joiner.

Strollin' Along

I was a "walker" to school. In the mornings I set off to the end of Prospect Avenue (now known also as Peter Falk Avenue, in honor of the actor who lived there) and turned to go down Clinton Avenue. Ossining is very hilly and Clinton Ave. was one of those undulating streets. Skittering down or huffing and puffing up were equally dicey when the weather was bad, particularly if there was ice.

I made my way to the high school, at which point I had to walk from the street to the back entry. There was a long sidewalk, one that was lined with a low wall and (stinky!) gingko trees. Kids would congregate there in small groups, talking and furtively dragging on that last cigarette before the bell rang. Reluctantly, I trod that pathway, head held down, looking at the pavement and crushed gingko fruit, certain that everyone was talking about me. It was like running the gauntlet—pure torture.

 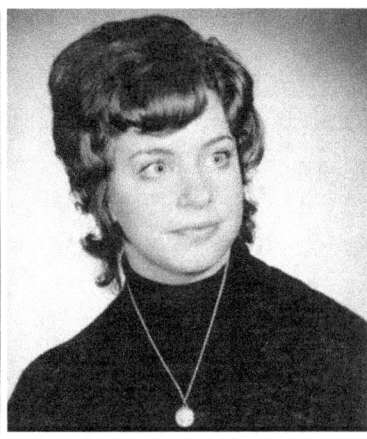

Yearbook pictures of me.

Lunchtime was not much better. A few times I would walk downtown to the luncheonette or pizzeria with Laurie or Sallie or Sally but mostly I sat by myself in the cafeteria. I was less aware of my aloneness here because I could read while I ate. In the nice weather I sat outside on the front lawn or the wall overlooking Highland Avenue and either read or watched the cars go by.

Rats! Foiled Again

Laurie was my best friend. I have a suspicion that her home life was as miserable as mine—one of the commonalities that brought us together. Come to think of it, perhaps the girls I hung out with all had dysfunctional families to one degree or another. Anyway, Laurie and I would spend time on the phone or at the steps of Ellis Avenue or at my place. (We rarely were at her house.)

One summer afternoon we were sitting on the back steps of my house, moaning about how we didn't have any cigarettes. "I have an idea," I told Laurie. "My grandmother always has cigarettes in her room; I'll go get us some." Little did I know that my grandmother was in her bedroom right above us. Since her windows were open she heard my ingenious plan.

I went in the house and up to her room. *Good, it's empty*, I thought. I tiptoed over to her dresser and sure enough, there was the pack of cigarettes. They were Kents—ick—but better a Kent than nothing at all. I picked up the pack and shook out two smokes. That's when I noticed the note on top of the cellophane. "14 cigarettes in this pack." *NO!* It dawned on me that Mom had come up with, in her understated way, a plan that would derail *my* plan. Laurie and I were out of luck.

An Education Revelation

At Mother Butler I had learned to smoke cigarettes and at Ossining High I learned how to smoke pot. I wasn't a big smoker—I only ever bought already rolled joints, never a bag—but I sure did like it. One time Sally and I smoked before our history class and we both got hysterical. I mean, even the blinds on the windows made us laugh. Our history teacher, Mr. Hunt, was lecturing and I found it hilarious. I just couldn't help myself. I think he knew what was up and kicked us out of class. I had to stand outside the door like a doofus which, of course, I found uproariously funny. He never reported us, though, so it all became a non-incident.

Monet or Midnight Cowboy and a Men's Motel

One Friday in the spring, our English class took a trip into the City. Mommy had apprised the school that I would not be returning with the group, since I would be staying at a relative's for the weekend.

As the bus wound its way around to the Metropolitan Museum of Art, we passed a cinema that advertised a showing of *Midnight Cowboy*. I had heard a lot of buzz about this film and decided this was more culturally interesting. Therefore, when we reached our destination I sneakily left the group to see my first and only X-rated movie.

It was a wild film, which I didn't understand. It was too outré for my 15-year-old brain, and although I naively considered myself so sophisticated, I couldn't make heads nor tails of the more "artistic" scenes so I left the theater with a modicum of cultural cachet but also a slightly bruised ego.

Once outside the movies I had to figure out a way to get to my great-aunt Louise's. I was not familiar with the transit system from the 50s on the upper West Side, and looked in vain for orientation. Which way should I turn to go south? Didn't really matter — it was too far to walk. I didn't see an entrance to the subway. After a block or two I came upon a depot with several empty buses. I trudged up the three rubber-covered steps of one, dropped money into the coin box, and took a seat. I was the only one on the bus; the driver didn't look once at me as I sat there in confused solitude. Why wasn't anyone else getting on? Why wasn't the bus moving? Which neighborhood was it going to?

It finally dawned on me that this bus wasn't about to go anywhere any time soon so I got up and, studiously avoiding eye contact with the driver, disembarked. Now I was really in a pickle. It was late afternoon and I didn't want to be wandering around once it got dark.

I came upon a hotel and decided to go in and ask directions at the front desk.

Striding up the steps I passed a few men coming out, and I entered the lobby from a revolving door. Funny, only men were in sight. Men who looked... unsavory. Missing teeth here, stubbly chins there, unkempt, mismatched outfits on many of them. The hair on the back of my neck slowly stood up. My mouth became dry. I beat a hasty retreat and decided, long or not, walking was the only option. I was beyond relieved when I finally reached Louise's and decided the best course of action was to say nothing on the experience.

The Park Lane Hotel

Plans had been made for me to stay at 50 Carmine since I had been offered a job in Manhattan and would spend weekends at Louise's. The job came about because my mother made friends with another teacher at Claremont, Joan Berger. Her husband owned a boutique pharmacy in Manhattan and had signed a lease to open a small satellite location at the newly opened Park Lane Hotel on Central Park South.

It was gorgeously appointed. The crème de la crème were the clientele, and it showed. Crystal sparkled and marble gleamed everywhere. Elevator doors slid open silently. Beautiful young men and women graced their positions at the front desk. Newspaper pages daren't rustle as they were turned. In short, this was the epitome of elegance. During a conversation between the two Joans it was arranged that I would work at the shop on the weekends.

After school on Fridays I normally took the train to Grand Central and then either bus or subway to the hotel. I would stay at Louise's Friday and Saturday nights then Sunday would return home. It was lovely of Joan and her husband to offer me this job and I blush to share that I did not do well by them. I was an opinionated, snotty teenager and I was not going to kowtow to the "snobs" who came in to buy their fancy cigars, heady perfumes, and foreign newspapers.

On the other hand, I longed to become part of this world, one in which grace and refinement were genetically bestowed. Accordingly, I dressed as well as I could during working hours, but upon leaving the shop I would go into one of the bathrooms (oh my goodness, they were stunning) and change into my "up yours" attire. Off would come the dress and kitten heels and on would go the jeans, tee shirt, and Timberland work boots. If it was chilly I'd add my Navy pea coat.

Joan Berger delicately mentioned to me that this was a very fancy, expensive hotel, blah blah blah, and that a certain mode of dress was expected. I nodded, and again, being a blockheaded teenager, didn't grasp the subtext. Too bad for me, because not long after it was decided my services were no longer needed.

Toe Shoes and Toilet Plungers

Mommy, my grandmother, Paula, and I were going to the ballet. But this was not the City Ballet of New York, nor was it a visiting troupe from Eastern Europe at the Met. No, we were going to a local production of *Giselle* at the old Scarborough Day School on Route 9.

In its heyday the well-trod boards of the building's stage had been graced by such luminaries as James Dean, Robert Frost, Julie Harris, and the King of Siam. Isadora Duncan had performed there. Our hopes were high.

We took our seats, folding and arranging our coats. Paula and I sat on ours to get a better view. The lights lowered. The crowd hushed. Parents of the young performers rutched in their seats, rustling the paper programs in anticipation. The tinny recorded music started, the curtains opened, and people oohed and aahed at their tutu-clad daughters on stage.

The young ballerinas twirled and performed their jetés admirably. Until one of them fell. Now you must understand that these were not the lithe, ethereal beings that floated across the stage as members of a professional company. These were mostly teens who loved potato chips and fries as much as they loved to dance. So when the Willis (their characters in the story) started to perform their wicked dance they also began to mysteriously fall to the floor. Most ungracefully. *Bang!* Another Willi hit the planks.

The first time it happened, the gasp from the audience filled the auditorium. The second time the gasp was slightly less audible. The third time, my grandmother and I started to giggle. The plight of the poor dancers was embarrassing, painful, and hysterically funny. At least to Mom and me.

My mother and Paula, both of whom had an exaggerated sense of propriety, scowled at us. This made us laugh even harder. I felt terrible! I truly sympathized with those girls but the spectacle was too comical for us to respond any other way. Mommy and Paula kept glaring darts and eventually our barely stifled snorting disgusted them so much that they got up and moved to different seats. We found out later that the surface of the floor had been improperly treated for ballet dancing and was too slippery, hence the collapsing of the Willis.

When the show was over and we all climbed into the car for the ride home, Mom and I got the proverbial tongue lashing from my mother. In true Mommy fashion, however, she turned the evening into a performance of her own. Mom and I were sitting on her bed and replaying what we had witnessed. Suddenly we heard clomping coming toward the room. My mother had turned into a Willi and was dancing down the hall. She was leaping up and landing deliberately flatfooted. Instead of a wreath of flowers on her head she sported a shower cap. And in place of a wand she imperiously brandished the toilet plunger. It is a sight I will never, never forget.

Louie, Louie

Mom's brother, Louie, a retired teacher, came to live with us. He had become a widower upon the suicide of his wife, Lucy. She was a sweet, gentle soul who, sadly, suffered with bone cancer. Louie was a parsimonious, self-absorbed, emotionally constipated man. So much so that when Lucy's medical benefits ran out, he refused to pay for any pain medication stronger than aspirin. I guess between the physical distress, as well as the emotional vacuum that was life with Louie, she finally decided she couldn't take it anymore.

He should have seen the signs. She pointedly asked him (we found out later) on which side of the chest the heart is found. She had very few possessions, none of which were worth much, but she wrote a list gifting particular items.

Then one fine day she walked to a neighboring field and shot herself in the chest, exactly where Louie told her the heart was located.

Funeral arrangements were made and Mommy and Mom attended. Lucy wore a simple flowered dress and a single strand of pearls. Her hair was in the usual soft bun, and her round spectacles were propped on her nose, just as in life.

During the visitation period Louie, sniffling and blubbering, walked up to my mother. He made the obligatory remarks about how sad it was, and how he was going to manage, and that he couldn't understand what had made her do it. Then he leaned in a little closer. My mother bent down slightly, because he was short, to hear what he was about to say.

"Do you think it would be OK to take the pearls off before she's buried?" he whispered. "It would be a shame to have them go to waste."

For once my mother was speechless. She gave him one of her "looks" (probably inferring, "you miserable, miserly bastard") and he slunk away.

During this period I was fitted with braces. My mother took me to the same orthodontist who had corrected Wendy's teeth, Dr. Perahia. His office was in Manhattan. We'd head up Rt. 9A, past the Cloisters, and into the Ft. Washington Area. For one appointment, Louie was asked to drive me since my mother wasn't available. He agreed, grudgingly, but with a litany of complaints.

At our return to Ossining, he decided he was hungry. We stopped at the Briarcade Diner, whereupon he perused the menu.

"Oy, everything is so expensive." He sucked air through his teeth and tapped his fingers on the tabletop, both habitual tics. I felt a twinge of guilt. He was nice enough to take me to my appointment and now here we were for lunch.

He went on and on about the prices to the point that when the waitress came to take our order I said I would just have a glass of water. She turned to Louie.

He said, "I'll have the spaghetti and meatball platter with Italian dressing on the salad. And extra butter for the roll."

He never made any indication that I should get something for myself. I sipped on my water as he chowed through his meal. When we got home I headed straight for the refrigerator.

It's a Grand Union

In lieu of joining any clubs or after-school activities I decided to get a job. Down Prospect Avenue and to the left on Croton Avenue was a Grand Union supermarket. One day on the way home from school I stopped in and asked for an application. The woman in the front office, Angie, handed me one. As I filled out the form everything was hunky dory until it came to the line that asked my age.

Oh jeez, I was only 14, and 15 was nowhere in sight. So I moved my birthdate by three years and made myself 17. Easy peasy and no working papers necessary. The store manager, Jay, interviewed me and… I got the job! I was also instantly in love with him. Jay was on the short and slender side, but that didn't matter to me. He had black, slicked back hair. He wore a white shirt tucked into tight black pants and Cuban heels. He was the epitome of cool.

I loved being a cashier. Maybe it tickled fond, long-buried memories of sitting on a counter at the dry cleaner's. Our registers had rows of buttons denoting the denominations for pricing. Oh, I was a whiz at it. In practically no time I had the prices of most things memorized and could slide those vegetable cans, bottles of milk, boxes of soap powder, packages of meat, paper bags of produce, and six-packs of beer right down the belt. I took pride in having all the bills in my drawer facing the same way and could make change like nobody's business. Training at the dry cleaners finally paid off. My bags of groceries were always neatly squared and if I had to double bag there were no wrinkles in the corners.

She Ain't No Friend of Mine

Florence worked in the deli. She was older and wore her black and silver hair teased and sprayed to within an inch of its life. She sported emerald green eyeshadow that demanded to be noticed. And whenever she finished shopping she would come to my line. Why? Because in those days customers could "earn" blue stamps depending on how much they spent. A large stamp represented one dollar and a small stamp denoted ten cents. These were spit out of a dedicated machine at each cashier's register and were separated with perforations. They would get licked and put in a special book. Upon accumulating enough stamps you could turn them in at the Blue

Stamp Store and pick out merchandise. (My mother actually saved up enough stamps to buy a beautiful grandmother clock, which today is in my daughter's living room.)

Florence had coerced me into giving her practically reams of stamps. She'd make some silly little purchase and then encourage me, "Come on, give me a few more. No, more than that. Come on, just a couple more." And I, too weak to protest, and too conditioned to acquiesce to an adult, kept my finger pumping on the damn button. Stamps came flowing out like perforated confetti.

The trick, though, was not to get caught. Every roll of stamps had to be requisitioned from the office. Angie would hand over a roll of large or small stamps, whichever was needed, but not before registering the stock number of the beginning stamp. Eventually it came to her attention that I was going through a ridiculous amount of rolls. If Florence and I had been caught I would have been the one to get canned. I was the one pushing out the stamps, which made me the perpetrator. Florence would have sailed on out of the store, "innocent" of any wrongdoing.

The full measure of Florence's character became clear to me when I was short on money and asked her to make me a sandwich (they did that at the deli back then). She *refused!* She said if she got caught giving me a free sandwich she could get fired. That's when I sadly realized that she was using me. From that point on I never gave her "free" stamps. It took a lot of fortitude on my part to stand up to her, but the injustice of the whole thing gave me the courage I needed to say "no."

Probably half of Florence's house was outfitted thanks to me.

A Hot Tomato

Emilio was the produce guy. People would select the fruits and vegetables they wanted and bring them over to wherever he was working. He would put the items in a scale that hung from the ceiling to weigh them. The scale had a round clocklike face behind glass and a thick black needle that spun around, slowly coming to rest on a number to indicate weight. Emilio would then scoop the contents into a paper bag while calculating the price. Taking the pencil from behind his ear he wrote the cost on the bag.

Emilio was a good looking guy for an older man but he creeped me out. He was forever asking me if I wanted a ride home, even though I lived only three blocks away. I never accepted.

One day I came home from school to find a letter addressed to me. Intrigued, I ripped open the envelope to find a single sheet of lined note paper. "I have watched you from afar. You are beautiful." And sentiments along those lines. My grandmother sat at the kitchen table with her usual cup of coffee and cigarette as I read.

I was baffled. Who was watching me? I felt excited at first, and then annoyed. Running through a short rolodex of possibilities in my mind I settled on Emilio. That letch! I then read the letter to my grandmother and indignantly told her I knew who it was. I said I was going to give him a piece of my mind when I next went to work.

I was ranting away when my grandmother started laughing. I stopped, mid rant, and asked her why this was so funny. "I wrote that letter!" she confessed. "You always complain that you never get mail so I thought I would send you some." I had to laugh, too. My grandmother did have an understated sense of humor, which rarely showed itself. It always took me by surprise. And thank heavens in this instance she came clean or I would have totally bewildered Emilio and embarrassed myself mightily in the process.

The Portuguese

While working at Grand Union I met Gus, a Portuguese guy. He was older than I was — and not particularly good looking, but he had this... *way*. One night he offered me a ride home and I accepted. It was dark when we left the store and he rumbled his muscle car up to my house, where he set the brake and let it purr in neutral. We started to make out, kissing and necking.

A heavy pounding on his window caused us to jump and break apart.

Oh lord, it was my mother. She was leaning over, laser beams shooting from her eyes. I shrank within myself. Poor Gus had no idea what he was in for. He rolled down his window and she started in. Her lips were stretched taut over her teeth. She looked positively lupine.

She concluded her tirade with, "If you are walking down the street and you see her, you had better cross over to the other side."

My mother never had to resort to yelling or raising her voice; the intimidation came from the control with which she couched her words. It left no doubt in your mind that she Meant Business and would Follow Through. That was the end of me and Gus. However, it was the start of my relationship with the Portuguese guys.

Gus had a group of friends, all Portuguese, who worked at the General Motors plant in Tarrytown. They had fabulous cars and were hot for American girls. Kathy was dating Armando, the oldest of the guys. Gus wound up with a girl named Mary, another co-worker from Grand Union. Sally and Sallie also were dating Portuguese guys.

I need to clarify. When I say dating, it was not the kind that meant going to the movies, or out to eat, or to the beach. It was under the radar kind of dating. These guys, all older, were very happy to date American high school girls — who thought they were so hip and wise but who had no idea they were being used.

One rare occasion when we actually ventured out during the daytime a group of us, in two cars, went to Playland at Rye Beach. On the way back the guys decided to race home. As we zoomed down the road I looked at the speedometer and we were going over 100 MPH! On the Taconic Parkway, no less, a winding, two-lane road! The two drivers were laughing and gesticulating, daring each other to go faster, to get ahead, to make that car in the front get out of the way. Tires squealed. The people we passed looked petrified. It was exhilarating and terrifying all at once. We had a great time.

I was introduced to a boy, Arminio. He was older too, but was shy and just off the boat, as they say. He didn't speak a word of English. Armando, the unofficial leader of the group, thought that Arminio and I should get together. And we did, for a while, but it was doomed from the beginning. First of all, there was the language barrier. Secondly, Arminio had been given the impression that all American girls "put out." This was reinforced during the evening four of us went to the drive-in. Armando and Kathy were in the front while Arminio and I were in the back. We started watching the film but before long the guys made their moves. In short order Kathy and Armando had gone full horizontal. Arminio, poor inexperienced, off-the-boat Arminio, tried to follow suit. I was having none of it. I guess I was a prude but I absolutely was not into heavy petting, or third base, or going all the way. Arminio resignedly gave up and we sat awkwardly in the back seat, unable to see out of the fogged up windows and forced to listen to the live soundtrack from the performance in the front seat. My relationship with the Portuguese — or as we called them, the "Porkchops" — ended soon after that.

My job at the Grand Union ended soon after that as well. I had orchestrated all the provisions for making my trip to California except for informing Jay that I would be gone. When I finally told him he was furious that I hadn't given him enough advance notice and fired me on the spot.

A Close Encounter

As so many teenage girls did, I earned money by babysitting and had some pretty steady customers. One evening I got a call from a Mr. Censullo, brother to one of the high school teachers. Someone had recommended me to him. I agreed to watch his two young children and walked to his house—he lived across the street from the school. When he and his wife returned he offered to drive me home. We got in the car and he started talking. I could tell he was kind of drunk.

On the way to my house, which was only five or so minutes away, he started coming on to me. I didn't know what to do! Some victims of abuse will react violently; others, like me, remain passive. I sat quietly in the passenger seat while my body stiffened into rigidity, like a turtle pulling its head into its shell. Thankfully he didn't get handsy, and when we reached my house I jumped out of the car. I never babysat for him again.

Reading, Writing, Refund

One afternoon I was alone in the house when the doorbell rang. I opened it to find a tall black man standing there. He was selling magazine subscriptions and before I could say anything he went into his sales pitch. I didn't want to offend him or hurt his feelings. (What if he doesn't meet his quota? What if I'm the last subscription he needs to meet his goal?) Again, the prey.

I agreed to buy, but I told him I didn't have any money on me, that I hadn't had a chance to pick up my paycheck. He offered to accompany me to get it. So, we walked to the store where I worked and I got my money. But it wasn't cash, it was a check. He then offered to walk with me to the bank so I could cash the check. We walked to the bank together and I paid him for the subscription. We parted ways and I went back home.

When my mother got home I told her about the encounter. She had a fit! Not that I had opened the door. Not that I had been walking around town with a strange man. No, she had a fit because I had been fleeced into buying some magazine! She was indignant and intended to get my money back.

She drove up and down the hills of Ossining, looking for a tall, well-dressed, black man walking around by himself. And to her credit, she found him! She launched into one of her diatribes. He countered her argument with the contract I had signed. She responded by ripping it up in front of him and held out her hand for my money. I'm sure he returned it posthaste, keen to escape the wrath of this crazy woman!

I wasn't there but I wish I had been; high drama is always entertaining.

Part of the Family

The job I held during The Great Magazine Debacle was at a butcher shop called The Ossining Meateria (to rhyme with "cafeteria").

One sunny afternoon on my way home from school I noticed a shop tucked between an accountant's office and a real estate agency. *I wonder if they need any help,* I thought. On an impulse I walked into the Meateria to see a woman at one of the two registers in the front of the store. I inquired about a job but she told me they weren't hiring. I asked her to take my name and phone number in case things changed. Less than a week later I got a call inviting me in for an interview. This same lady, Sylvia, was married to the owner, Louie. She asked me about my experience. I assured her I knew how to work a register and talk with customers. Right on the spot she hired me!

I joined Louie and Sylvia's two daughters, Carol Ann and Lisa, who also worked part-time, as well as Louie's nephew, Steve. Irene was the full-time female employee. (Her husband owned the liquor store in downtown Ossining. He was always referred to by his nickname, Goo Goo; I never learned his real name.) Two other women worked there from time to time; Rose, who became a friend of mine, and Rina, Rose's sister-in-law. Sometimes Liliana, Rina's niece, would fill in. Gary, nicknamed Mooney because of his round face, was a butcher with a pronounced stutter. Lisa, Steve, and Sam, Gary's younger brother, were classmates. A third butcher, Tommy, a hot-tempered guy, rounded out the full-time staff.

Working at the Meateria was a wonderful experience. I loved being part of a family business and I liked all my co-workers. It was all very cozy and I almost felt like I finally found somewhere that I belonged.

That's a Wrap

In addition to working the register I also became a "wrapper." The Meateria was quite a busy store and a lot of meat was pumped out of the back room. Whole, half, and quarter carcasses were delivered straight from the meat market in the Bronx and the butchers would "break them down." The chops, steaks, ribs, roasts, chickens, and hamburger meat were put into Styrofoam "boats." Trays of the boated meat would be given to the wrappers, who manned one of two stations.

The wrapping machine was a small table with a steel surface. The boat would be put on the top tray and plastic wrap from a large roll under the table would be brought over and under the boat. A hot wire would cut the wrap, and then both ends would be sealed up. There was an art to pulling the plastic wrap with the right amount of pressure to fold under the boat. The final step was to plop the boat onto a heating pad that sealed the plastic tight. If a piece of meat was big enough, or shaped in an unwieldy manner, it was up to the wrapper's discretion whether to double-wrap. This process was an exacting science that demanded a high level of speed, accuracy, and professional discernment. And I prided myself on being fast, accurate, and discerning.

Genoa or Hard?

I also worked the deli. This involved slicing cold cuts, weighing out salads, and keeping the case, slicer, and scale neat and clean. One day an older woman asked me for half a pound of "Italian" salami. Now I knew there were two salamis, Genoa and hard, which we also called Jewish salami but I was confused as to which salami fell into the "Italian" category. I asked Irene if she knew which meat I should slice. She looked at me like I was a little bit daft. "Well, the Genoa salami, of course. Whaddya think?" I answered her — in all seriousness — "I wasn't sure cuz there are Italian Jews, you know." I couldn't understand why that made her laugh. In my mind that was a perfectly reasonable point. So I sliced the lady's "Italian" salami and she went on her merry way. Another satisfied customer.

A Rose is a Rose

Rose was married but had no children, which may explain why she took a shine to me. A big-bosomed woman with an impressively towering teased coif, she was a hard worker with a soft voice. On the nights we both worked until close she would drive me home, even though it was a fairly short walk from the store to my house. Once parked out front we would often sit in the car, talking. Talking long enough that Rose would turn off the engine. Eventually my mother was uncomfortable with this.

"What does a grown woman have so much to talk about with a 16-year-old?" Mommy snorted. "What does she want with you?" Suspicion was always lurking in my mother's mind.

"She doesn't want anything!" I was incensed. "We just talk about all kinds of things."

My mother wasn't convinced.

"Well, I don't like it. Tell her she should at least come in the house."

I had no plans to do that; it would have been so awkward.

Being only 16 I had not yet developed a sense of tact. The next time Rose drove me home I told her I couldn't stay to talk. Naturally, she wanted to know why. Forging ahead like the artless teenager that I was I told her that my mother didn't like it. I believe Rose was hurt and insulted, but the damage was done—I could not take back the words. Happily, Rose didn't hold my mother's mistrust against me. I continued to visit at her house and to be friendly at work.

Rose was such a generous person that she allowed me to borrow her car. I do not say this lightly—she owned a fire engine red, hot off the showroom floor, 1969 Dodge Charger, and could that thing growl its way up the road. The few times I drove it I was exhilarated but also scared out of my wits. It had so much power, and its hood was about as long as an aircraft carrier. But she trusted me with it and I did my best to deserve that trust.

One Foot into My Future

One day as I was working the register, a red-headed man walked through the door and directly into the back room. I heard raised voices. As I later found out, his name was Pete. He came in to discuss an incident that had happened over the weekend. He and Louie both belonged to the same club (either the Elks, Sons of Italy, or the Columbus Lodge).

Pete had tried to get into the club with a friend of his, who was black. Apparently guests were allowed, unless they were black. A ruckus was raised over this and Pete had come in to hash it out with Louie, who had some pull. Pete was incensed that his friend had been treated poorly and wanted to settle the score, or at least straighten things out. The resolution was immaterial—I was bowled over by Pete. I was in awe that he would stand up for a friend of his to such a degree.

He wasn't very tall but he had admirably broad shoulders and biceps that bulged in his jacket. As it turned out, he was Tommy's older brother and was a butcher as well. And oddly enough, he wound up working there. As I later learned, there was quite the circle of butchers in Ossining; they rotated steadily between the three shops in town. Pete had been working for a guy named Tony but eventually moved over to Louie's shop.

As intimated earlier, I found Pete very attractive. Not only was he nice looking, but I was so impressed by the stand he took on behalf of his friend, particularly at a time when race relations were tenuous at best. I admired his (very public) willingness to defend his friend's right to be admitted to the club. Loyalty and fortitude have always been important to me.

So I kept my eye on this Pete. And it seems he kept his eye on me, since not long after he started working there he asked me out. I was smitten! On Cloud Nine! Here was this older guy—by seven years—who drove an Olds 442 (take *that*, you Portuguese!), was handsome, and best of all, principled. I had never been asked out before and the night of our date seemed centuries away.

But of course it eventually arrived. I heard his car pull up to the curb of our house and waited for his knock at the front door. Instead, he honked the horn. *He must be in a hurry*, I thought as I ran out to the car. I hopped in and we smiled at each other. Pete was taking me to dinner, to Izzy's, a great little local Italian restaurant that sat close to the Hudson River. I ordered lasagna but my electric tingle of nerves and excitement were so palpable, so discomforting, that I couldn't eat. I cut the lasagna into bite-size pieces and rearranged them about the plate, hoping Pete wouldn't notice that very few of them were going in my mouth. His appetite was unaffected, though, and he finished his meal as we made small talk. The rest of the evening is a blur.

Come Blow Your Horn

As happens with a new relationship, the tight bud opens slowly and the bloom becomes more fragrant, more vibrant. The stem grows taller and stronger. But... the stars in our eyes block out the insidious start of a weed that slowly, imperceptibly, peeks up out of the soil to see where it can ensnare and strangle the unsuspecting flower.

One fine spring day we decided to go to the Bronx Zoo. The sky was a thin aquamarine, a promise of the deeper azure to come later in summer. Trees budded and birds twittered their joy at the warmer temperatures. We strolled along the pathways, stopping here and there to watch the animals. As we were paused in front of one display I felt Pete's arm drape casually across my shoulder. It seemed so natural, so right. That casual gesture intimated protection, ownership, security, and I leaned into his body. On the ride home, we said very little but the car was full of unspoken emotion and promise. We belonged together.

We planned another date, and as before, Pete honked the horn and I hurried out to the car. I opened the passenger door and hopped in. I noticed that he was still wearing his work boots, and there were small bits of meat clinging to them. Never mind, this time we were going to the movies!

Another date and again, the honk from Pete's car summoned me. This time, however, my mother intercepted.

"He should come to the door to get you," she remonstrated. "Go out and tell him he needs to come in and meet me."

My cheeks were red and my voice wobbled a bit as I approached the car from the driver's side. "My mother would like you to come in," I managed to say with a little bit of a smile, hoping to soften the blow.

Pete pulled the car to the curb and turned off the engine. He walked with me to the door and we went in. I didn't know what to expect, and I imagine he didn't either. But thankfully my mother was perfectly cordial, and as they shook hands and made pleasantries my racing heart rate returned to normal. Actually, I was surprised that my mother hadn't given him the third degree and then "laid down the law." After a few minutes we left the house and were on our way.

Our dates continued, but now Pete was always careful to come to the door to collect me. At some point he met Mom, who seemed less enamored with him. I believe she thought I'd be better off with someone closer to my age (Pete was 23; I was 16), who wore clean shoes and respected me enough to call at the door unbidden. In retrospect, I understand that she was disapproving but said nothing. The hierarchy of our household had been well established and she held her tongue.

An Unmet Expectation

As our dates became more frequent Pete became bolder in his treatment of me — our own rules of hierarchy were being established. One incident remains fixed in my mind as particularly curious and unpleasant. We were at the drive-in and in those days when couples went to the drive-in there were certain unspoken… expectations. Pete made clear what he wanted and I was not willing to accommodate. After Pete put himself together he got out of the car and took a pee at the bottom of the back tire. So many emotions sprang to the surface; I was infuriated and upset and confused all at the same time. And disgusted. Who does that? I got out of the car, intending to walk home, even if it was in the dark and miles away. Pete started up the car and began to follow me.

"Where are you going?" he asked through the open window.

"I'm going home," I replied. I kept my pace steady and looked straight ahead to show I meant business.

"What's wrong?" he asked.

I didn't answer.

"Come on, get in," Pete said. "You can't walk home—it's too far and it's dark out. Get in!" he entreated.

"No. I'm walking home."

We went back and forth but eventually I relented. This time, the car was filled with an ugly cloud of silence and discomfort. When we got to my house I wordlessly got out and went inside.

If I had grown up with a sense of self-worth, a strong sense of self-respect, my life might have gone down a completely different road. But as it was, I continued to see Pete, and the Drive-in Incident was never mentioned. As time went on, however, my resolve weakened and Pete mostly got his way. I remained too enamored. The stars in my eyes never dimmed and I fell deeper in love with this man. And I believe—no, I know—that he loved me too. My mother, as well, became increasingly approving and accepting of Pete.

There actually were times when he visited at the house, and remained long after my mother and Mom went to bed. He would stay over and we would sleep together in my single bed. With him so close I felt safe and immune from the chaos of my family's day to day life. The yelling, screaming, tears—or even worse, the chilling silence between my mother and grandmother—faded away as I nestled securely into Pete's arms and drifted off to a peaceful sleep.

Sneaking Off

When I was a junior, as the weather became nicer I became less inclined to sit in class. But what to do? I certainly couldn't hang around the house since my grandmother was always home, and what was the point of walking around the few blocks that constituted "downtown" Ossining? The city of White Plains was my salvation. It was a bus ride away, and it had boutique stores and dinettes, and… a Macy's! I had money burning through my pocket and White Plains seemed the perfect place to lose it. But what would be the mechanics of it all?

Skipping school was no problem but returning to class presented its challenges. How would I explain my absence? Let's see. I could forge a letter from my mother. No, too risky. I would never be able to sustain her handwriting for an entire note. (I never stopped to think that no one was going to perform handwriting analysis on it.) But wait! I *did* imitate her signature pretty well. If I could only get some blank excuse forms that I could sign…

These forms were in the office of the Dean of Girls. Could I? Would I? Dare I? Yes! I waited until I knew for sure the Dean would be out of her office and then helped myself to a few sheets off the pad. Thank goodness CCTV hadn't been invented yet. So here and there (gotta spread the days out; don't want to raise any suspicions) I took myself to White Plains and had a ball. Glorious freedom! In and out of shops. Perusing the counters at Macy's. Hamburger and fries and the luncheonette.

It sure beat the heck out of geometry.

Them Tires is Smokin' – and so were we

After my stint at the Meateria I got a job in the meat department at Finast supermarket, which was a good mile away from home. So I wouldn't have to walk my mother bought me a car – my very own car! Actually, walking *to* work wasn't a problem but walking *from* work in the dark worried her. So I became the proud owner of a Ford Falcon. It was white with a red interior and I couldn't have been happier.

One afternoon Kathy and another misfit friend, Tommy, and I ditched school and took a ride in said Falcon. We went to one of the local parks where I backed into a hidden rut, and we lit up, and I don't mean Marlboros. It had poured the night before and whatever wasn't grassy was puddles of mud. Including the little lane in which I had parked.

When we decided it was time to leave we got in the car.

I started it up.

I put it in drive.

I stepped on the gas.

And we went nowhere.

I revved the engine but the tires just spun uselessly. Kathy and Tommy got out of the car and went around the back to push while I continued to gun the accelerator. In our chemically induced state of hysteria we naturally were falling over laughing at our predicament. So I mashed the gas pedal, the tires spun, and Kathy and Tommy got covered in the mud that spewed from under the tires. We laughed even harder. I don't know how the heck we got out of there but somehow we did and went on our way.

The last time I smoked weed was not so funny. A group of us went out one rainy night and we were pretty high. Which meant we were pretty hungry. At the Briarcade Diner we ordered hamburgers, fries, and Cokes. After we devoured that meal we decided we were *still* hungry and someone suggested we go across the road to Arcadian Gardens where there was a pizzeria. Pizza — what a brilliant idea!

So we piled into my car. After waiting for the traffic light to turn green (thankfully I had enough sense to obey the red light) I turned into the Arcadian parking lot. However, I misjudged where I was turning and ran over the concrete divider that separated incoming and outgoing traffic. I didn't realize what I had done but in my juiced up state I thought I had run over a pedestrian. I was in a complete panic and sobered up immediately.

My heart raced and my mind instantly conjured up the scenario of my impending murder trial, facing my mother, being sent to prison. I determined then and there that I would never get high again. And except for one incident years—decades, actually—later, I never did. Other friends eventually graduated to experimenting with LSD and even heroin, but my days with drugs were over.

A House Divided

Around this time an incident of nuclear proportion took place. My sister, my poor sister, who was held under my mother's thumb like a bug squashed between two glass slides and placed under a microscope, was at the breaking point. Paula met with her school's guidance counselor, who was alarmed enough to request an appointment with my mother, who worked in the elementary school across the street.

When Mommy arrived home after the meeting she slammed through the front door like a hurricane, her face twisted with fury. All three of us—Paula, Mom, and I—visibly shrank away from the ferocity of her anger. She was ranting and raving: how dare Paula spill our family life to a stranger! How dare Paula complain after all she (Mommy) has sacrificed for us! She, who has always done her best for us! How dare Paula cry about the "terrible" things she has done to her! And on and on. Not one of us said a word. My mother ended her tirade with an announcement that since she was such a terrible person she didn't deserve to live with us in the regular part of the house so she was moving to the attic.

To the unfinished, uninsulated, unheated attic.

Mommy proceeded to move all her things, requisitioning my assistance. Together, we moved her dresser around the angled corner of the door leading to the attic, and up the stairs, but she dragged and pulled her mattress, box spring, and bed frame by herself. She then piled all of Paula's belongings into the newly emptied room. I can't imagine the fear and regret and pain my sister was experiencing. Was she worrying about what would happen in the days to come? Was she anxious about any other repercussions? To my shame those concerns never crossed my mind; I now had the bedroom to myself and selfishly, I was glad.

Moving On Up

I enjoyed my solitary room for a good long while, but then my uncle Ronny came to stay with us. Ah, my uncle Ronny. I was still besotted with him. I recoil at the remembrance of it now, but at the time I had this fixation with him. Did it have anything to do with a clear memory of when I was a little girl?

A set of stairs in a semi-lit apartment building, standing beside a man in duck pants who was sitting on a step grasping... something erect and unfamiliar... in his hand.

To show how much I esteemed him I offered up my precious room. And he took it. This man usurped the bedroom, my haven. At the time I was honored to have made this gift, but from an adult standpoint I see this was wrong. He was the adult and should have made other arrangements. He was working in the Bronx and therefore was only home in the evenings. He had enough money to rent a place (he was only planning to stay a couple of months before moving from the area) and had no financial constraints. But never mind. Move into my room he did.

So where did that leave me?

In the attic with my mother. The unfinished attic. Separated from the rest of the house. Sweltering in the summer heat. Making sure not to impale my head on any of the nails protruding from the rafters. Wiping off the dust from the unfinished floor powdering my feet before getting into bed. Stacking the rolled up posters from my walls in a corner. Setting up my little record player on an old unused chair (at least there was electricity). Lining up my teenage store of perfume, talc, hair spray, makeup on an unfinished board. I made that part of the attic "mine" as best as I could.

Eventually, as planned, my uncle left to move on. My room was empty! I had plans other than moving back into it, though. Haunted by my mother's litany of injustices against her, I resolved she should have her own place. So one day while she was out, Pete and I moved all her things from the attic into my old room. We set up her bed and dresser, put her clothes in the closet (up in the attic she had strung up clothesline on which we hung our clothes) and generally made it look comfy.

When she came home, my surprise set her off and she blew the proverbial gasket. She ranted and raved about how she didn't deserve her own nice room (this was all iterated sarcastically), she wasn't a fit mother, and so forth. Another free ride on the Guilt Train Express.

As she was raging she hurled all *my* stuff down the stairs. Clothes, bedding, books, records, pillows, shoes, all came flying down into a big heap at the bottom of the staircase. Pete was there at the time and I was utterly humiliated that he witnessed this unbridled insanity. Silently stuffing tears of hurt and anger down my throat in soundless gulps I picked up my belongings and put them into the room. Later, after Pete had left and the three of us were in the kitchen, my mother told Paula and me that we were not to call her "Mommy" anymore, that we were to address her as "Joan." She didn't want to be our mother any longer.

The cherry on top of the dysfunction sundae, made especially just for us.

1972

Pete

The romance between Pete and me deepened quickly. I would even call him from the phone booth at school between classes so I could hear his voice. I think the infatuation stage in most relationships is defined by these little moments that just the two of you share, but in my case the infatuation was coupled with believing I had a protector, a man who was as capable of standing up for me as he would an interloper in a private club. Also, I was so unhappy at school that having a man of my own—a man!, not a schoolboy—gave me something that I couldn't get anywhere else: Stability. Safety. Assuredness. Knowing that at the end of the school day that if Pete was off work he would pick me up in his 442. A man's car. Oh, how every minute away from Pete felt like an eternity. Like I was rudderless, blowing this way and that, however the wind pleased.

I believe he felt the same way. His home life was as unstable as mine—still living with his dysfunctional parents and brother Tommy. I think he felt a sense of peace in our relationship because when we were together, either physically or on the phone, we were cocooned and away from the tempest both our families created. But we were young and immature, damaged people who were trying to create their own world, one of peace and normalcy.

But what was normal? We had never known it.

I did not see the dysfunction in our relationship, the inability of either of us to make reasonable future plans, the incapacity to get to know each other on a deep level, the total lack of understanding of how to successfully navigate an adult world and to forge our place in it. Instead, we were bound together by physical attraction, momentary pleasure, and escape from both of our broken families.

It's in the Cards

Ralph Brophy was Pete's best friend, even though he was older, married, and had four kids. We had spent many fun, long evenings with the Brophys, playing pinochle. We would have marathon games that could last until 1:00 or 2:00 in the morning.

The Brophy house was a small Cape Cod; as one entered the side door (the only door anyone ever used) you stepped into the dining room, which was only big enough to hold a table and chairs. The hutch was actually located in the living room and was filled with Waterford crystal. But that was not the only crystal; an ornate chandelier hung over the table. Sadly, because Ralph, Pete, and I smoked, it was perpetually veiled in stale cigarette smoke. Anyway, we four would sit around the table, puffing and shuffling, dealing, and laying down cards. We often fortified ourselves with wedges (what others might call hoagies or subs), or leftovers that Diane, Ralph's wife, would scrounge up from the fridge. Chinese take-out was a treat. During one epic session we even boiled lobsters!

It's All Fun and Games Until...

The Brophys were famous for having rollicking parties, and many of them. It was amazing what Diane could produce from her claustrophobic kitchen. Downstairs, Ralph manned the wet bar. One summer day, party season in full swing, Pete and I found ourselves invited to one such get-together.

I was in a terrible state. I didn't know what to wear. I was still so intensely self-conscious about my looks; I always felt inferior, less-than, insecure, and would inwardly damn myself for all my deficiencies. This occasion was no different.

After trying on and discarding numerous outfits — and combinations thereof — I conceded to an *au courant* pair of hot pants. But my legs! They were so pale. I resolved that problem by wearing pantyhose under them. What to wear on top? This white blouse? Too stark. This short-sleeved sweater? Too hot. This tank top? My bra strap might show. I eventually settled on a flame-stitch patterned ruched pullover. *At least any fat around my middle will be hidden*, I sighed to myself. I slipped into platform sandals, inserted big hooped earrings, and made my way down the stairs and into Pete's car. He had been waiting patiently for quite a while.

Off we went and 10 minutes later parked at the end of a long line of cars in front of the Brophy house. It wasn't that hot a day but I was sweating already. Damn! The pantyhose cast off an unnatural sheen in the sunlight. It was kind of humid, so I hoped my hair wouldn't frizz too much. I shouldn't have worn sandals, I should have put on flats. But they would look ridiculous with hose. *Look at all these cars… I won't know half the people here. Do these earrings make me look "cheap," as my mother would say?* Carefully clomping down the steep driveway I held onto Pete as we went in to join the throng.

I was right. I didn't know most of the people there, and to make matters worse, they were all old enough to be my parents! I pasted on a smile and wove in and out of little groups, trying to look like I knew where I was going and what I was doing. I clutched a cup of soda (Scotch and I had yet to be acquainted. We would meet disastrously on New Year's Eve) and finally plunked myself down on a picnic bench.

As the party progressed, Pete drank more and more. Ralph was already half in the bag before we even arrived. I made my way to a folding table that boasted the buffet. Standing there I tried to decide what I wanted to eat.

WHAM!

Something hard hit me forcefully in the middle of my back. Tripping, I momentarily saw stars. I steadied myself on the edge of the table and turned around to see Ralph holding a long loaf of French bread like a baseball bat. He was laughing uproariously. I looked for Pete and there he was, right behind Ralph, laughing right along with him.

"That wasn't funny! That hurt!" I said, hoping they didn't notice the wavering in my voice.

They laughed even harder.

The pain in my back subsided but the hurt in my heart was a stab in my chest. Why did Ralph do that? Why was Pete laughing? Why didn't he protect me, protest what had happened? I stood there for a moment, stunned and confused.

"It was just a joke," Pete managed to get out between inebriated laughs.

"Take me home," I stated firmly. The hurt had given way to anger.

"Oh, come on, Ellen. Can't you take a joke?" Pete said, now sounding annoyed.

I turned and went into the house. What was I going to do? I didn't want to stay there but I had no way to get home. I didn't have money for a taxi. I couldn't call my mother; she never liked Ralph. I decided to call Pete's brother. Thankfully Tommy was home and agreed to come get me. He arrived soon after and took me home. I hadn't eaten at the party and I felt empty inside. But it wasn't the emptiness of hunger, and food would not have filled up this hole.

Happy New Year

It was December 31, 1971, and we were to meet the Brophys for a New Year's bash, to be held at the Ossining Armory. This was my first formal event. Thankfully, Wendy, my fairy godmother, immediately took charge of my wardrobe. We went into Manhattan to Lord & Taylor, a department store that catered to upscale clients. This was not just a store, it was an experience of understated elegance. Beautiful lighting from chandeliers. Mirrored floors. Saleswomen standing at attention. Goods in spotless glass cases. And gowns. Lovely, splendid, sublime gowns. We examined each one carefully—me with a marveling eye, Wendy with a practiced one. The choice was difficult, but I settled on a peacock blue, floor-length sheath overlaid with a silk chemise of blue and green and black swirls. It was sleeveless and had a plunging back. Shoes next (heels, of course) and a delightful little sequined handbag completed the ensemble.

The day of the dance, Diane did my hair (she was a beautician, as we said back then). I applied my makeup and since I had a blemish on my back, Paula carefully applied makeup to cover it up. The butterflies in my stomach were fluttering up a storm; I was in a high state of anticipation, edgy excitement, and worry all at once.

The hour arrived—it was time to leave. Pete came and looked so handsome in his suit and tie. The sky was ebony velvet with diamonds winking down at me, promising a magical evening. We got to the Armory, Pete with one hand holding mine and the other grasping the neck of a bottle of Johnny Walker. Coming closer to the entrance, the pulse of live music enticed us to hurry up. We found the Brophys and joined them at the table.

The room swirled around me—gowns, cigarette smoke, music, perfume, laughter, colored lights… Pete poured me a drink, his go-to, Scotch and water. I took a sip and, oh lord, it was awful. But I was determined to throw off the taint of teenage-hood and assume the mantle of "adult" so down it went. And another. *Oh good! Here comes our dinner.* Rib eye and potatoes and a vegetable medley and Scotch. Have a cigarette! *Yea! Time for the Bunny Hop.* And another Scotch. *You know what? It actually doesn't taste that bad.*

5, 4, 3, 2, 1. *MIDNIGHT!*

"HAPPY NEW YEAR!"

Confetti. Kisses. Music. Whistles. Horn blowing.

What, time to leave? OK.

I serpentined to the car, accompanied by Pete's amusement at my condition. Oh, I was in sorry shape. (Pete was in fine form himself.) Slumped in the seat I waited for Pete to start the car — I needed to get home. The RPMs of the 442 made my stomach roil. We got on the parkway and Pete made for my house. Every curve in the road made my head roll and my stomach lurch.

"I can't go home like this," I slurred. "My mother will kill me."

"I'll take you to my house," Pete replied. "You can wait 'til you feel better then I'll take you home."

At this juncture we were on Yale Avenue, a notoriously windy, hilly road. That did it.

"Pull over, I'm going to throw up!"

I was in a panic. There was no way I was going to make it to Pete's house, even though it was less than five minutes away.

"Hold on, we're almost there," he encouraged.

"I can't! Pull over!"

I frantically rolled down the window.

Well, he didn't and I did.

Except I didn't get my head all the way out the window. New Year's Eve dinner and a whole lot of Scotch blasted partly out the window and partly between the door panels. Vomit dribbled down the front of my Lord & Taylor, handmade-in-Spain gown. My stomach settled down somewhat and sudden exhaustion steamrolled over me.

Meeting Viola

We pulled up to Pete's house. It was dark; everyone was asleep. We got inside and Pete steered me into his bedroom, which was actually the master, meaning it had its own bathroom. I went in and turned on the light. Who was that in the mirror staring back at me? Some poor bedraggled girl with mascara blotching her face, red eyes, and a lopsided bun on her head. *Oh lord, there's no way I can go home looking like this.* I was so very tired. *I'll just wipe my face, lie down a little bit and then Pete can take me home. Mommy will never be the wiser.*

As I see-sawed across the room I began to divest myself of clothing. I wobbled out of my shoes, the heels of which had poked holes in the hem of my gown, and left them in the doorway of the bathroom. I wriggled shakily out of my pantyhose, which lay where I dropped them. I shimmied my dress to the floor, retrieved it, and threw it thoughtlessly on a chair. Now clad only in my bra and panties I crawled over Pete, who had already passed out on the bed. I lay on a pillow—a blessed, soft pillow that cradled my swimming head—and gave into oblivion.

I heard a noise.

Faintly.

There it was again…

I peeled an eye open and a short, round figure gradually came into focus.

"Petie, wake up! Wake up! Petie! Who is that?"

A very small, rotund, gray-haired woman was trying—most unsuccessfully—to rouse Pete.

Nothing seemed to register in my brain. *What time is it? What is going on? Who is that person?*

There's no way I can deal with this right now, I decided, and I closed my eyes and went back to sleep.

And that is how I met Viola, my future mother-in-law.

A Ring and Roses

February rolled around and Valentine's Day made its appearance. Pete came over to the house, a shy grin on his face. He sat me in a living room chair and… proposed to me! He carried a gorgeous bouquet of red roses. He bent on one knee and opened a box in which was cushioned a stunning one-carat solitaire cut diamond ring. I had never seen anything so beautiful. It was flawless and sparkled with promise. Without hesitation I replied yes.

We had talked about getting married and treated it as a foregone conclusion—we were madly in love!—but this time-honored formality made it official. And although my mother had seemed accepting of Pete's presence in my life, I did not know how she would react to this turn of events. After all, I had only turned 17 the previous November.

Instead of reveling in the moment, maybe having champagne, my family around me to congratulate us, I hustled Pete out the door. I had no idea which Mommy would receive this news, the raging, manic one or the lockjawed, silent one.

My mother must have heard the front door close because she came into the living room looking puzzled. "Did Pete leave already?" she asked.

"Yeah, but he gave me this," I answered.

I thrust the little box in her hand and made my way out of the living room ASAP.

"It's beautiful!" I heard her gasp from the kitchen.

Timidly I made my way back into the living room and looked at the ring with her. It was dazzling. I slipped it on my finger, delighted to see that it was a perfect fit. My mother looked genuinely happy and I was genuinely relieved.

The next morning I couldn't wait to get to school. I had to show the girls! I was gratified when I heard their *oohs* and *aahs*. The lights in the gym made it sparkle spectacularly. I couldn't stop looking at it.

I was a senior in high school and an engagement ring graced my finger. The irony of my derision toward engaged classmates in Colorado never crossed my mind.

I showed it off to our gym teacher, Mrs. Justice. Her reaction was quite different. Surprise? Shock? Doubt? I couldn't read her expression but was unconcerned.

"You're gonna marry who? Pete Stay-sigh-ack?" laughed Mr. Crawford, my Social Studies teacher, deliberately mispronouncing the last name. "I knew him. Certainly not the student his sister was."

"You'll be divorced in five years," predicted Mr. Bardari, my English teacher.

You're all wrong, I thought defiantly. *I'll come back in five years and show you all!* All the negativity and misgivings in the world could not damper the glow I felt. Well, except for one person's. My grandmother's lack of enthusiasm prickled me. Couldn't she see how happy I was? Why was she so quiet about my impending marriage?

Please, Mom, be happy for me.

Wedding Plans

My mother had a discussion with Pete and me about the actual wedding date. She said we had two options: we could get married the upcoming June—of course I wanted to be a June bride—and have a small wedding, or we could wait one year and have a bigger wedding. We didn't need much time to think about it, we were in a hurry! So it was decided that the wedding would be that June, 1972, the year of my high school graduation. Time was short as June was only a few months away, so action had to be swift and decisive, my mother's favorite modus operandi.

Invitations were designed and set for printing, on ivory paper with hand-torn edging and gold embellishment.

A cake was decided upon at the Briarcliff Bakery—orange sour cream cake with vanilla buttercream frosting.

Dunstun's dreamed up a beautiful design for flowers.

I was set on a honeymoon in Aruba but our travel agent talked us into going to Jamaica.

Dresses! We needed one for me, naturally, and then one for Wendy, who was to be my maid of honor, and one for Paula, who would be my bridesmaid, and one for my little cousin Jeanine, who would be my flower girl. (Lavender, they have to be lavender.)

Mommy took me to Macy's in White Plains, my erstwhile hooky stomping grounds. We rode the escalator to the bridal department where we met with a bridal consultant. She showed us an array of beautiful gowns, all of which, depressingly, were out of our price range.

"Well, we do have some that are on sale," the consultant advised us. "They're on a rack in the sale department."

"We'll take a look at those," my mother smiled back, concealing her relief.

The consultant led us past the pricey, out-of-reach gowns into a back room that was painted the sickly green of a rundown hospital. Oily, black dust gathered in the corners. Overhead pipes clacked and burped occasionally. The rejected gowns were hanging forlornly on a rack as promised. One by one Mommy slid the hangers across the rack, creating the groaning protest of metal resisting metal. She stopped at one. It was an A-line of satiny fabric with some lace embellishing it. The veil was a little crown with lots of illusion fabric cascading down past the shoulder.

The consultant eagerly assured my mother. "That was a very popular design. We sold many of them and this is the last of the lot. Sadly, we had to move it back here to make way for the new designs coming in."

My mother looked at the price tag. "Ellen, why don't you try this one on?" she encouraged.

As I emerged from the makeshift dressing room I looked at myself in the mirror. I looked beautiful! My mother was ecstatic. It fit. It was available. There were no imperfections.

And that is how I came to be married in a $99 wedding dress.

I'm a Good Little Soldier

One day, toward the end of May, Pete suggested that we take a day trip.

"Well, okay, but it's pretty hot out. What did you have in mind?" I asked.

"Let's go to West Point," he replied.

I wasn't too keen on the idea but I agreed. "Let me change first," I conceded.

So off we went to West Point, about 30 minutes away up the Bear Mountain Parkway. We parked and walked around the visitor's center, the museum, the campus, and then up to the fort. By the time we returned to the car I was hot, exhausted, and thirsty. I couldn't wait to get home for a drink, a change of clothes, and to turn on the fan, and lay on my bed.

Taken by surprise.

"*SURPRISE!*"

Bewildered, I looked around the living room. What were all these people—these women—doing here? Why were my mother and grandmother dressed up?

Oh my goodness, it was my bridal shower! I was totally taken by surprise. I looked at Pete, standing behind me with a conspiratorial grin on his face.

"Is that why we went to West Point?" I laughed.

"Your mother told me to take you out for a few hours, so yeah," he smiled back.

Opening wedding shower presents.

It was a great afternoon (after I cooled off!). We had a lovely buffet, lots of chatter, and of course, presents. I was "showered" with generosity—so many gifts that were needed to start a married life. I still have many of these items some 50+ years later, and I can recall every person who gave me each one.

The Day Arrives

Preparing in front of my grandmother's mirror.

Finally the Big Day arrived. June 17th. I was to become a Mrs.! Oddly enough I didn't feel jittery. I actually felt calm. Again, Diane did my hair. She washed and conditioned it in her kitchen sink. I sat on the folding stool underneath the kitchen phone on the wall as she created an ornate twist and made sure the veil would sit on it properly. Once home I carefully applied my makeup and gave myself a goodly spritz of perfume. Slowly, gently, I lowered the wedding gown over my head, being careful not to muss my hair. Did someone help me button up the dress? Attach the veil? I'm sure they must have but I don't remember. I eased my toes into a pair of low satin heels. I gave one last look at myself in the mirror and made my way down the stairs.

Wendy, Paula, and Jeanine were ready and waiting in their lavender and ivory gowns. My uncle Bobby was waiting for me, handsome as ever in his suit, ruffled shirt and all. He would be driving me to St. Augustine's in Pete's car (Ralph, as best man, was driving Pete). Bobby was also going to walk me down the aisle. I was proud to be on his arm but I thought of someone else the whole time. How I wished it could be my father performing this ritual. I felt his absence keenly.

Looking hopefully to my future.

We arrived at the church and after carefully extracting myself from the car I made my way to the front of the building. Standing on the sidewalk I waved at passing cars that honked at all of us gathered by the front steps. It was a beautiful, perfect June day. A cerulean sky without a single cloud.

Wendy, me, Paula, and my little cousin Jeanine.

Holding the hem of my dress high I climbed the stairs and went into the cool of the nave.

Escorted down the aisle by my uncle, Bobby.

As my eyes adjusted to the dim light I inhaled the warm scent of incense.

I heard soft music wafting down from the organ loft.

I saw friends and family turn and stand and acknowledge me.

I saw the white bridal path stretched out before me.

Pete waited for me at the altar.

My new life was to begin.

Epilogue

I only ever wanted two things in my life: to be a mother, and to be a teacher. When it was time for me, as a Catholic girl, to be confirmed, I chose for my confirmation name "Anne." She was the mother of Mary and I reckoned that she must have been an extraordinary mother if God chose her daughter to bring Jesus into the world. I wanted to be that kind of mother, one who would raise her children in such a way that God would be infinitely pleased with them.

When I was pregnant with my first baby I had the obligatory baby shower. So many adorable things! Hopes and dreams and expectations wrapped and beribboned in yellow or green gift paper. (This was before the days of learning the sex of your baby before birth. Hence, no pink or blue.) Unbelievably tiny sleepers. Velvety receiving blankets. Crib sheets festooned with lambs gamboling through rosebuds. Adorable rattles and squishy teethers.

But when hopes and dreams and expectations collide with a lifetime of dysfunction and abuse, any idealism that pipe dreams foster is destroyed.

The infant years of my children were marked by sweetness and supreme happiness. Breastfeeding was hands down the most enjoyable experience of my life. Skin to skin, downy cheek to full breast, a soft mouth, cuddling a sleeping baby who, as my mother said, was "drunk with milk." Such a precious, intimate time that was just between my baby and me. Oh, I was "drunk" with joy and promise.

But life is not a hazy, dreamy fairy tale. We are not promised a happily ever after. Actually, after… what? Illnesses, sleepless nights, paychecks stretched tighter and tighter… Couples who were raised in families defined by acceptance, love, forgiveness, and the absence of abuse are equipped to weather the storms that inevitably are a normal part of life. These people are emotionally healthy, prepared to ride out trials, and actually emerge stronger and matured.

I was not raised in such a family, was not emotionally healthy, and had no sense of who I was, what I was doing, or where I was going in life. My husband and I lived day to day, without thought of the future. Nothing in our pre-married lives had given either of us a healthy sense of self; we were all id with neither ego nor superego anywhere in sight. We were two people with plenty of unresolved — heck, unrecognized — anger and with no idea of how to deal with it.

For my part, this anger was a feral, untamable animal that I was helpless to master. Frustration would build to an unmanageable pitch and to my everlasting shame I so often alleviated the pain by screaming and cursing. During these episodes my mind would be yelling at me: *Stop it! Get a grip!* I would see the fear in my little children's faces but be absolutely powerless to control myself. Did I feel better afterward? No. I felt worse. On top of anger I now had guilt to grapple with. Additionally, I felt mortification as a sinner and betrayer of the trust God had placed in me by giving me children.

For years I had felt spiritually unfulfilled as a Catholic. I did not believe in the infallibility of the Pope. I disagreed with the notion of confession — why did I need to "confess" to a priest? Didn't God already know my failings? I had long since given up praying to saints or to Mary. I would attend mass with high hopes (especially those with extra pomp and circumstance, like Midnight Mass) only to leave after the service feeling empty and unsatisfied.

Then my baby died. My first baby.

Jon's death was totally preventable. The fault lay directly at the feet of the obstetrician who refused to come to the hospital, even after the nursing staff contacted him — three times! — to inform him the baby was in distress. (My husband and I were completely unaware this was the situation.) By the time the doctor deigned to show up it was too late. The umbilical cord had strangled Jon and he was pulled from my body, dead. He was whisked away and I never got to see him or hold him.

Around this time I had started (sporadically) attending a local independent Bible-believing church. It was a small but very active congregation. When the believers there learned what happened, their response was overwhelming. My husband and I received many letters in which people shared not only their condolences but their own experiences with grief of one kind or another. Their honesty and willingness to be open with two people they barely knew brought Pete and me to tears. Meals were delivered. People stopped by just to offer a hug. One gentleman in particular came by every day after work, for two solid weeks, just to sit and talk with us to help fill up what would otherwise be a dark, empty hour. In short, these beautiful people demonstrated the love of Jesus. I realized this is what I had been searching for—a *relationship* with God, not a *religion*.

I began attending Calvary Baptist Church regularly. The young pastor and his wife took us under their wings and discipled us. (Pete had also declared his belief in Jesus as Savior.) I eventually decided to make a public profession and was baptized. As each of our subsequent children was born, four in all, we dedicated them to the Lord.

This should have been the beginning of not only my spiritual growth but emotional as well. But just as Dorothy was instructed to "pay no attention to that man behind the curtain," I paid no mind to the anger that was always simmering just below the surface—even as it boiled over and spilled out. I devotedly attended services on Sunday mornings and evenings and Wednesday evenings, studied my Bible, forged friendships with other young Christian mothers, and even opened our home to a Bible study once a week. But I struggled on a regular basis to mature into the Christian mother and wife that I wanted to be. I felt weak and ineffectual and a failure. I think an apt analogy would be one wherein a person suffers a broken leg, goes to the doctor, and is fitted with crutches but the bone is never set. In other words, if the root injury is not addressed then the broken body will never heal completely or correctly.

And that was my problem. I fragmented myself. I recognized my spiritual self and my physical self but never understood there was also an emotional self. This disassociation persisted for decades, until I was in my 40s. That is when God brought a Christian therapist into my life. I had always loved writing but it took Bonnie to show me how to use words as a tool to understand myself. Through countless hours (and pages!) of journaling I began to glean that my childhood and adolescence had not been "normal." I was able to understand my family's history of abuse and dysfunction that informed my mother's psyche and subsequent behavior, and therefore mine. I was able to finally comprehend the source of my rages and learn how to mitigate them. Bonnie talked with me, prayed with me, and at times held me, and little by little put me together.

This was a humbling and very painful time. I felt sad for myself, to be sure, but the realization, the coming to grips, of the harm I had done to my children over the years wrought in me a pain that was palpable. I prayed earnestly for God's forgiveness and wrestled with accepting that He understood me—after all, He created me!—("Before I formed you in the womb I knew you…" Jeremiah 1:5) and graciously, lovingly removed my sin "as far as the east is from the west" (Psalm 103:12). The hard part was—and at times still is—exonerating myself.

I have gone to each of my children and asked them for forgiveness. I have apologized. I have worked to make up for lost years. But I wondered, *Do they understand? Can they truly forgive without appreciating* why *I was* who *I was?* And thus the idea for a memoir was born. I have recounted my remembrances (not definitively—here and there something else will come to mind, but maybe those lagging memories are for another volume) for the purpose of trying to bring about an understanding of what my childhood was like. More than anything, I want there to be healing and completeness.

My fervent prayer is that this story, my story, will bring peace and complete restitution between my children and me. I pray that the years of my life in which my proclamation of faith in Jesus was made a lie will be mitigated. I pray that my children — and any reader — will see that God is able and faithful to restore that which has been broken, the years that the locusts of anger and dysfunction have eaten (paraphrasing Joel 2:25). And finally, I pray that you, dear reader, will see that if we earnestly seek forgiveness, wholeness, peace, and joy, God is pleased to bless us with such.

"If you then, being evil, know how to give good gifts to your children, how much more will your Father who is in heaven give good things to those who ask Him!" (Matthew 7:11)

Acknowledgments

There are a few people I would like to acknowledge; it is a short but mighty list.

To my dear husband, George, whose battle cry "FTB!" (Finish the Book!) often propelled me to my laptop when motivation was not to be found. Your gentle prompting and consistent encouragement kept me committed to the goal I had of writing a book. You unselfishly gave me time to myself, and many nights suffered through a simple sandwich or bowl of cereal for supper so I could keep writing. I don't say it often enough but you are my rock. I love you.

My editor, Demi Stevens, just like the lions at the NYC Public Library, personifies patience and fortitude. She deserves to be conferred with sainthood! Over the course of many emails, texts, and cups of coffee, she took a sloppy first draft and crafted it into the beautifully finished product you hold in your hands.

Peter Stasiak, whom I marry at the end of this memoir, recognized my love of writing and unstintingly supported me in that endeavor.

Lia Allen, cheerleader par excellence, thank you for believing I could actually pull this off and for checking up on my progress periodically.

Jamie Wilkins of Capture All Moments Photography came through at the 11th hour to shoot hundreds of pictures for me to pick one for the back cover. Thank you for working your magic—you make me look good.

To the English Department of York College of Pennsylvania, particularly Dr. Edward Jones and Dr. Gerald Siegel, my deepest thanks for encouraging this insecure, 40-something student in a classroom full of "kids." You gave me confidence and the belief that I actually had some small talent.

I owe Bonnie Renn Smith an enormous debt. You took this broken woman, whose life was teetering on the brink, and put me back together, piece by piece. Your wisdom, guidance, and love led me to a path of healing. I am forever grateful.

My mother, Joan, has departed this earth but her influence remains a living constant in my life. She showed me what grit and gumption are. She taught me to be generous and giving to others. She taught me to read when I was four years old. She sat with me on our couch and recited poetry aloud, even though at the time I didn't quite "get it." She introduced me to the achingly beautiful librettos of opera. Mommy, you were my first and most important inspiration. I wish you could have been happier. But you gave me what you could, and for that I bless you.

Finally, and unreservedly, I acknowledge my Father in Heaven. You gave me the courage to dredge up long-buried memories and recount them with clarity and honesty. When I was stuck for a word You whispered it in my ear. You gave me wisdom as to what to include—as well as what to delete. I thank You and praise You for being beside me every step of the way on this journey. You are a good, good Father.

www.ingramcontent.com/pod-product-compliance
Lightning Source LLC
Chambersburg PA
CBHW052132070526
44585CB00017B/1801